#startupeverywhere

Startup Guide Miami

EDITORIAL
Publisher: Sissel Hansen
Editor: Marissa van Uden
Proofreader: Josh Raisher
Staff Writers: Charmaine Li, Shelley Pascual
Contributing Writers: Matthew Speiser, Phineas Rueckert, Mario Ariza and Andrew Boryga

PRODUCTION
Production Manager: Eglė Duleckytė
Project Manager: Allison Lubarsky
Researchers: Allison Lubarsky, Lucas Baker

DESIGN & PHOTOGRAPHY
Designer: Ines Pedro
Photographers: Zak Tassler, Antonio Tarin, Daniel Arrondo, Fabio Delo

Additional photography by Ryan Song, CodeArt, Florida International University, LaunchCode, Wyncode Academy, Miami Dade College, Miami Herald, Ines Pedro, Refresh Miami, Home61, David Sutta Photography & eMerge Americas, Chris Klula, Unsplash.com

Illustrations by Joana Carvalho
Photo Editor: Daniela Carducci

SALES & DISTRIBUTION
Head of Sales: Marlene do Vale marlene@startupguide.com
Head of Business Development: Anna Weissensteiner anna@startupguide.com
Head of Distribution: İrem Topçuoğlu irem@startupguide.com

Printed in Berlin, Germany by
Medialis-Offsetdruck GmbH
Heidelbergerstraße 65, 12435 Berlin

Published by Startup Guide World IVS
Kanonbådsvej 2, 1437 Copenhagen K

info@startupguide.com
Visit us: startupguide.com
@StartupGuideHQ

Worldwide distribution by Die Gestalten
Visit: gestalten.com

ISBN: 978-3-947624-10-2

STARTUP GUIDE
MIAMI

STARTUP GUIDE MIAMI

In partnership with **Knight Foundation**

Proudly supported by

Sissel Hansen
/ Startup Guide

Most often associated with sun, sand and parties, Miami is so much more than that. The city is gradually transforming itself into a place synonymous with startups and innovation. In the Kauffman Foundation's 2017 Index of Startup Activity, which examines new business creative activity and people engaging in startup activity across America, the Miami-Fort Lauderdale area topped the list at number one among forty metropolitan areas. Not only that, Miami was also selected by Amazon as one of twenty finalists that could be potential hosts for its HQ2 site.

Instead of replicating the Silicon Valley way of doing things, Miami is carving its own path as an innovation hub by playing to its set of strengths. In addition to a lower cost of living (especially when compared to cities like New York and San Francisco), the city boasts a diverse population, balmy temperatures and close proximity to the Latin American market, which makes it an ideal place for entrepreneurs looking to scale their businesses internationally. With Art Basel and the Wynwood Arts District, let's not forget about Miami's bustling art scene and the international creative crowd it brings into the city.

In the past couple of years, new accelerators and incubators have cropped up in the city to boost startups of all kinds, including Startupbootcamp Miami for the digital health sector, 500 Startups Miami with its programs for entrepreneurs at various stages and LAB Miami Ventures, which caters to an array of sectors. Undeniably, the John S. and James L. Knight Foundation has played a crucial role in Miami's ascent as a tech center by investing in local entrepreneurial initiatives that strengthen the community, such as Endeavor Miami, eMerge Americas and Refresh Miami, as well as bringing big names into the city. One thing that makes Miami stand out is the way different players in the startup ecosystem have banded together with the mission of building a better future for all entrepreneurs – a true community effort.

As Miami's startup scene continues to heat up, we can't wait to delve into the community and explore the entrepreneurs, coworking spaces, accelerators and experts shaping the city's startup scene in the first-ever Startup Guide Miami.

Sissel Hansen
Founder and CEO of Startup Guide

Francis Suarez
/ Mayor of Miami

Miami, which is often referred to as the "Magic City," has gone from being a gateway city to a global city. This is not only because of our wealth of diversity and multiculturalism, but also because of a unique entrepreneurial spirit that resonates deeply through our neighborhoods. Innovation has become just as much a part of our community's fabric as the warm nature of our people and weather, characteristics that lie central to our city's identity.

To progress in what is a disruptive and ever-changing world, cities must embrace technology. Miami is leading the way as a forward-thinking city that is harnessing innovation and forming strategic partnerships to enhance our residents' quality of life, solve problems and prepare for the jobs and challenges of tomorrow. Today, we are seeing the results. According to the Kauffman Foundation, Miami ranks number one in startup activity. As a world-class destination with perfect weather and a low tax environment, Miami has become a premier destination for companies seeking to relocate, plant their roots, grow and diversify.

To solidify Miami's position as a dynamic entrepreneurial hub, we have partnered with several companies and events including eMerge Americas, Endeavor Miami and StardomUP. These initiatives nurture our tech scene by boosting our intellectual talent through mentorship, education and funding. In addition, we are using technology to protect our residents. With ShotSpotter and Ring, we are integrating crime-prevention technology into our police department's existing resources by providing officers and residents real-time, local crime-and-safety information. We have also collaborated with coworking spaces like WeWork to facilitate business growth for startups and established companies alike through interactive communal workspaces.

Thanks to these efforts, Miami continues to send a strong message that we are open for business. Our city stands as a key player in the knowledge-based economy that is attracting innovators from around the world. With Miami's international reach, we are ideally suited to continue nurturing our diverse community of entrepreneurs, who propel our stature on the world stage as a vibrant epicenter of opportunity and growth.

Francis Suarez
Mayor City of Miami

Local Community Partner / Knight Foundation

Miami is not new, but it feels brand new. It is not officially the capital of anything – not of Latin America or of Florida – but it is where two continents meet. Miami is a bridge between cultures – a city of makers, visionaries and strivers. It's where the American Dream comes to life, and it happens every day of the week.

Miami welcomes all, but it's not a place for everyone. If you are not truly comfortable with diversity, or if change intimidates you, don't come. Do come if you want to create and to embrace what's just around the corner. Do come if you have a dedication to innovating and improving. That is the nature of our city.

At Knight Foundation, we are social investors who fund opportunity. We look for ideas in community that have the potential for transformative, sustainable impact. That's why we've invested $150 million in the arts over the last decade, helping Miami transform from the winter home of Art Basel into a year-round arts town.

It's also why we invested in Miami's budding entrepreneurial ecosystem. It was a natural opportunity in our city of small businesses and immigrants. Our community sought a future where talented graduates could stay and thrive, where anyone could bring good ideas to life. They sought a future where world-class innovators could connect, collaborate and create lasting change for Miami and beyond.

This book shows that Miami's future is now.

A few years from our initial investments, entrepreneurial activity is booming. Our focus now is on helping ventures scale, especially in industries where Miami is uniquely positioned for success, such as health, logistics, finance and tourism. We're also supporting avenues for underrepresented communities and new residents to take advantage of our city's growing innovation economy.

Miami is a city for those who dream big and work hard. It's where you come for the palm trees and stay for the possibilities. The contents of this book are both a roadmap and an invitation for you to take part in Miami's new era.

Welcome to our future.

Alberto Ibargüen
President and CEO, Knight Foundation

contents

STARTUP
GUIDE
MIAMI

Local Ecosystem

- Miami is experiencing a tech boom, advancing past its reputation as a hospitality and real estate economy.
- Magic Leap, a virtual reality startup based just outside of Miami, raised $2.3 billion to become one of the country's top startups.
- 500 Startups, a $400 million Silicon Valley investment fund, chose Miami as the place to open its new East Coast office in 2018.
- Florida is #1 in startup density, #3 in established business ownership, and #4 in the rate of adults becoming new entrepreneurs in the US.
- Miami is #1 for concentration of coworking spaces due to the massive influx of startup activity.
- Miami-Dade County is a hub for international commerce and culture with a 52 percent foreign-born population and a 68 percent Hispanic population.
- Florida is one of only seven states in the US that has no state income tax.

- Magic Leap raised $963 million between October 2017 and March 2018.
- Origis Energy raised $100 million in November 2016.
- CareCloud raised $31.5 million in November 2016.
- Boatsetter raised $14.5 million between December 2016 and June 2017.
- Neocis raised $15 million in June 2017.
- Willing raised $7 million in November 2016.
- itopia raised $5.5 million between October 2016 and June 2017.
- Home61 raised $4 million in October 2017.
- Wyncode raised $1 million in February 2017.
- ChronWell raised $5 million in February 2018.
- Plum raised $10 million in May 2018.

Sources: cbinsights.com/research/well-funded-startups-us-map; miamiherald.com/news/business/ article216037720.html; kauffman.org/kauffman-index/rankings; miamiherald.com/news/business/ article201883369.html; census.gov/quickfacts/fact/table/miamidadecountyflorida/POP060210; stateofflorida.com/taxes.aspx; crunchbase.com; census.gov; bls.gov/regions/southeast/summary/ blssummary_miami.pdf

[City] # Miami, United States

[Statistics:] Miami-Dade Population: **2,751,800**
US total population: **328,620,000**
Miami-Dade unemployment: **4.3%**
US unemployment: **4.1%**

Intro to the City

While Miami is traditionally known for white-sand beaches and salt-rimmed margaritas, the city has been slowly shedding this image over the last decade as intentional shifts have been made by local leaders and newcomers to inject the city with innovative startups, arts and culture and a burgeoning tech industry. In 2017, a nationwide report measuring startup activity, opportunity and density of entrepreneurs rated Miami as the top city among forty others.

There's also a wide range of support from local government and deep-pocketed foundations to support these new businesses and help them get their vision off the ground (last year, Miami startups received $1.3 billion in venture capital funding, ranking it in the top ten nationwide). In short, what was once a city to party in is rapidly transforming into a robust city in which young, hungry entrepreneurs and innovators have many opportunities to work just as hard as they play.

Miami is the largest city in the sunshine state of Florida and consists of a diverse variety of people and cultures. The greater metropolitan region, known as Miami-Dade County, is divided into a number of small cities such as Miami, Coral Gables, Miami Beach and Hialeah, among others. Each has its own distinct flavor and vibe, but all live under the larger umbrella of Miami-Dade, or "the 305" as locals affectionately call it (an ode to the local area code).

Before You Come

Although Miami is part of the US, Spanish is extremely prevalent, so it would be a good idea to brush up on beginner language lessons before you arrive. Salsa lessons probably wouldn't hurt either. If you're moving to Miami from outside of the US and plan to stay longer than three months, you'll need to acquire a visa prior to your arrival. This process could take anywhere from three to five weeks. If you're coming from a country with harsh winters, leave your coats, scarves, gloves and hats behind and bring sandals, swimming trunks and floral outfits in their place. The vast majority of days in Miami will be sunny and above 80 degrees Fahrenheit. Winter in Miami constitutes 60 to 70 degrees Fahrenheit on any given day.

Cost of Living

As interest in Miami has grown and the city has attracted more people, the cost of living has risen. Among one hundred metropolitan areas in the US, Miami was ranked as the forty-first most expensive in 2017. Although residents in Miami earn less on average than residents in cities like New York, the lack of income tax in the state of Florida often equates to Miamians earning similar wages as other big-city dwellers after taxes. However, housing is not cheap, and you should expect to pay upwards of $1,800 for a suitable one-bedroom. To stretch your budget, aim to live close to centers of transportation, such as Downtown Miami, Brickell, Midtown or Coral Gables. Living near public transportation will also allow you to avoid the second-biggest expense when living in Miami: a car.

Cultural Differences

Miami-Dade County is home to the largest share of Hispanic or Latinos (68.6 percent) of any major US metropolitan area. Unlike other similarly diverse cities, most Latino residents in Miami are recent arrivals to the US or not far removed from family members who immigrated. In many stores, restaurants and shops, Spanish is more common than English. Don't let this intimidate you. Miamians are warm people who appreciate a good-faith effort to grasp the Spanish language, and most residents speak both languages. In addition to a large Latino population, there are large African-American, Haitian, Jewish and Russian communities. All of these groups blend together in a wonderful cocktail and make for a wealth of cultural and dining options to explore. One activity that many residents unite and rally around is sports. Miami is home to three major professional sports teams: the Miami Heat (basketball), the Miami Marlins (baseball) and the Miami Dolphins (American football).

Renting an Apartment

Miami is growing rapidly with many new condos and rental units, so finding an apartment in a desirable area should not be challenging. In Miami, renters and buyers do not pay real estate agents for their services; instead, agents are paid by the buildings and properties they direct you to. This often results in agents taking you to properties they have a relationship with and helping to negotiate on prices (tip: always negotiate on prices!). Nonetheless, it wouldn't hurt to do your own research. Reputable sites include zillow.com and apartments.com. Both sites present a range of properties as well as agents who can help schedule viewings and answer questions. Also check out Roam Miami (roam.co/places/miami), a beautiful coliving space in Little Havana. For areas close to transportation with good dining and entertainment options, and for buildings that combine living and coworking space, look at Brickell and Downtown Miami. For those into the arts and the hipster scene, Wynwood is a popular destination. Family-friendly areas include Coral Gables and Coconut Grove. Little Havana is culturally rich and famous for its Cuban culture, but still affordable.

See **Flats and Rentals** page **228**

Magnus Sodamin
@magnificentmagnus

Finding a Coworking Space

For many Miamians who work in the startup scene, the innovative workspaces and opportunities to interact with other entrepreneurs are crucial to thriving. Luckily, Miami has a growing number of coworking and flexible office spaces. WeWork has a large presence, with locations in Brickell, Coral Gables and Miami Beach. For those who work in the tech space, the CIC Miami is a place to rub shoulders with many innovators in the local industry. It also hosts many weekly events and incubators for those looking to network and grow their businesses. The LAB Miami is a trendy coworking space in the center of the Wynwood arts district, and home to many events connecting the tech and arts communities.

See **Spaces** page **76**

Insurance

Healthcare in the US is undergoing constant reforms. As of 2018, it is mandatory to have health insurance; however, the mandate that requires uninsured Americans to pay a fine expires in 2019. Nonetheless, it is advisable that you purchase insurance in the US, as medical costs can be expensive and insurance can drastically offset out-of-pocket expenses. If you're living in Miami on a visa, you can choose a health-insurance option from the healthcare marketplace (visit **healthcare.gov**).

If you plan to own a vehicle in Miami, it is mandated by the state that you purchase an auto insurance plan. Non-citizens and citizens alike are eligible for the same plans. Reputable companies that offer affordable options include Geico, Progressive, Allstate and Statefarm. To keep costs lower, consider paying up front for six months of coverage at a time rather than month to month.

See **Insurance Companies** page **229**

Visas and Work Permits

Before moving to Miami, consider how long you plan to stay in the city, as this will determine what visa to acquire. For less than ninety days you don't need a visa. If you plan to stay for longer, you can apply for a business visa that lasts for up to three years. To be eligible, you must have attained a bachelor's degree or your nation's equivalent degree. You also must have experience in a "specialty occupation," defined as a job that requires theoretical and practical application of specialized knowledge in selected fields. For some fields, state licensure to practice may be required. Foreign employers seeking to establish a new office in the US are also eligible to apply for a visa under certain conditions. For more permanent stays, there are five visas you can qualify for based on whether or not you have family living within the US, your work experience, your nationality, and your plans for investment within the US. To find out more, visit the US Department of State website at **state.gov**.

See **Important Government Offices** page **229**

Taxes

Filing your tax return in Miami is relatively simple, and there are many locations available to handle your needs. A range of professional tax-filing companies is available to walk you through the steps needed to file. Unlike in most US states, Florida does not charge a state specific tax. The only taxes you'll be required to pay are federal taxes. The US tax system works in brackets, and charges those who earn more a higher percentage. If you hold self-employed tax status and are paid by clients who do not deduct taxes from their checks, be sure to put aside at least 25 percent of what you earn in order to be prepared for your tax bill at the end of the year. In the US, the window for filing annual taxes begins January 29 and ends April 15.

See **Accountants** page **228**

Starting a Company

When starting a company in Miami, there are a few steps you must follow. The first is to choose your company type: for-profit, non-profit or limited liability (LLC), depending on which one best fits your business. You must then register your business with the Florida Department of State (**sunbiz.org**). This step requires you to provide information about the scope of your business, ownership and employees. A small filing fee of $100 will be required. After this, you'll have to register your business with the IRS. This will provide you with an employer identification number (EIN), which is used when filing federal taxes. Registering your business with the local Department of Revenue is not required by law but is advisable in order to protect your business name from being used elsewhere in the state. Finally, check the Florida Department of State Division of Library and Information Services to find out if you need a license to operate your business. License fees range from $50 to as much as $500, depending on the scope. To find information about the city's startup scene and networking events, *The New Tropic* is a useful publication. Finally, check out funding opportunities in the form of grants from local organizations such as Knight Foundation, the Miami Foundation and South Florida Angels.

See **Programs** page **60**

Opening a Bank Account

Opening a bank account is a priority as soon as you arrive in Miami, as bank statements are often used as criteria to judge loans, suitability for apartment rentals and more. There are low-fee banks, such as Barclays and Ally Bank, that operate without physical spaces in Miami. Reputable banks with many ATM locations and brick-and-mortar offices around the city include Bank of America, Chase, Capital One and Wells Fargo. While you can open an account online or over the phone as a foreign visitor, it may be helpful to visit a physical location to learn about the full array of options at your disposal. The specific criteria required for opening an account at each bank varies, but generally you'll need proof of a foreign or local address in the form of a utilities bill or other mail, a passport and a driver's license.

See **Banks** page **228**

Getting Around

Although Miami is a growing and bustling city, the infrastructure for transportation has been slow to catch up. If you live in the metro areas, such as Brickell, Downtown and Midtown, there are a number of free transportation options you can take advantage of, including the light-rail Metromover and the network of Miami Trolleys. Both options are reliable, but service a relatively small area. The Metrorail spans further and will connect you to desirable areas such as Coral Gables and Coconut Grove, as well as get you quickly and efficiently to the Miami International Airport. A ride costs $2.25, but there are monthly packages available.

The bus system has spotty service and long wait times. Rideshare apps such as Uber and Lyft are popular and affordable for local trips. However, if you live outside of the surrounding metro areas, having your own car may be more efficient. Miami traffic is particularly dreadful during the morning and evening rush hours. If possible, try to live in an area with access to transportation so you can avoid it altogether.

Phone and Internet

AT&T, Verizon, T-Mobile and Sprint are some of the reliable telephone providers with excellent network coverage in Miami. They offer a variety of packages for both personal and business use. Affordable alternatives include MetroPCS and Cricket Wireless. Prepaid cell phone options exist, but if you're staying in the city for the long term it would be best to set up a more permanent arrangement. Some companies have plans that allow you to pay month to month, but most require a contract that lasts anywhere from twelve to thirty-six months. In general, you should expect to pay between $40 and $100 a month, depending on your data and accessory needs. Payment for most companies can be made online through credit cards or checking accounts.

Learning the Language

Achieving basic fluency in Spanish will make life easier for you in Miami. Local institutions such as Miami Dade College, Florida International University and the University of Miami offer continuing education classes for new Spanish learners that range in length from an intensive seven days to once or twice a week classes spread over a few months. Class times are flexible and include night and weekend offerings, and they can range in cost from $1,000 to $5,000, depending on the institution. There are also smaller, more affordable language academies such as the Gaviria Academy of Languages that offer pay-as-you-go sessions for as low as $20.

See **Language Schools** page **229**

Meeting People

Miamians are a friendly bunch and you should have no problems meeting new people if you're open to different cultures. Your best bet would be to hit networking events as well as trendy areas for bars and nightlife in neighborhoods such as Wynwood, Brickell and Little Havana. Some popular bars in the city center include Wood Tavern, Ball & Chain and Blackbird Ordinary. For those interested in the arts, there's the Perez Art Museum in Downtown, monthly art walks in Wynwood and the Miami Book Fair held every November in Downtown Miami. There's also the internationally famous Art Basel, a two-week art experience held in December in different locations around South Beach, Wynwood and Downtown Miami. In addition, there are networking services such as IVY and Miami Under 40, which offer opportunities for young professionals to meet up for fun events.

See **Startup Events** page **229**

ups

[Name]

Addigy

[Elevator Pitch]

"We're a software platform that allows traditional companies to elevate their Apple devices in the IT ecosystem."

[The Story]

No matter who you are or what your workspace, chances are you might use an Apple product at your job. As Apple products become more ubiquitous, Addigy is bringing specialized IT support to companies around the world that use them. The platform allows administrators to secure, update and manage these products remotely, all through a simple pay-as-you-go model. "Traditionally, Apple devices are the black sheep in an organization," says Jason Dettbarn, founder and CEO of Addigy. "There was a whole cloud ecosystem of software to help IT manage PCs, but on the Apple Mac side, there was nothing. Other people thought this was a small space; my gut told me that this was a massive space. And because there were no other companies in this space, I saw this as an opportunity."

Jason's bet paid off. In the past year, Addigy's revenue has shot off the charts. More than six hundred companies around the world – in the US, Middle East, Europe and Australia – now use Addigy. "We decided we can make a simpler platform and do it for a space that is absolutely underserved," Jason says. "If you walk into Best Buy, every Mac uses Addigy; tech companies like Lookr and Robinhood.com use us; we serve everything from big organizations to small, nimble companies."

[Funding History]

Bootstrap

Up until now, Addigy has been completely bootstrapped through revenue. "Our mindset was not finding cash, but putting in the time to get it right and not rush it," says Jason. Now, however, the company is at a point where it can leverage its capital into potential investment.

[Milestones]

- Increasing revenues tenfold in the past year.
- Building a remote team of sixteen people, with offices in Miami and Portland.
- Surpassing six hundred clients around the world.
- Instituting a strong workplace culture and providing world-class benefits for employees.

[Links]   Web: addigy.com Facebook: addigy Twitter: @addigy

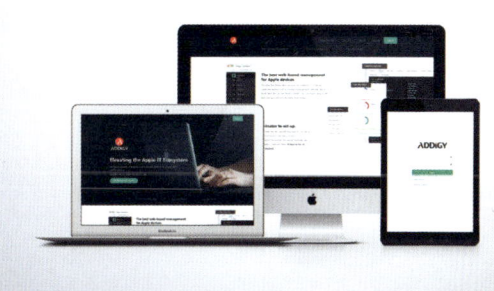

[Name]
Blanket

[Elevator Pitch]
"Our mission is to automate personalized outreach - to help companies generate elegant one-to-one messages for every potential customer, at scale. We build tools that help companies scale the way they prospect, connect, score and convert their leads."

[The Story]
Blanket, an online platform that automates the process through which companies book sales demos, came about as the result of a well-timed pivot, a little bit of luck and a wealth of deep connections within the Miami ecosystem. Founder Alex Nucci initially created the platform to fill a need he experienced while building another company, Gramercy, an online referral platform for ecommerce companies. Because he couldn't afford to hire a full sales team, he decided to eliminate the need for one by automating parts of the sales process. The result, Blanket, quickly developed into the bigger story. "I looked at all the things sales teams did and started productizing," Alex says. "We kept building and building this product, and it kept converting better and becoming more interesting. Eventually, it became a larger product opportunity than Gramercy.io."

Still in its beta stage, Blanket builds customer profiles for businesses, prospects thousands of leads, drafts and sends out personalized emails to potential customers and finally brings customers to individualized landing pages where they can sign up for the product, book a demo or fill out an interest form. "Our goals are pretty lofty," Alex says. "We think we can change almost everything about sales and marketing. It's a huge market and a huge business opportunity, and we are approaching the problem in a very unique way."

Seed   Angel   External

[Funding History]
Blanket's initial investment came from a small cadre of VC and angel investors in the Miami ecosystem, including Mark Kingdon and Miami Angels. Alex was later invited to join the spring 2018 cohort of investor Jason Calicanis's LAUNCH Incubator in San Francisco, where Blanket brought on initial customers. The company is currently raising a seed round from institutional investors.

[Milestones]
- Realizing the product was not just "shiny object syndrome" and pivoting away from Gramercy.io.
- Raising $640,000 in funding to-date and bringing on a good number of paying customers.
- Building a remote, global company while maintaining Miami as our home base.
- Being invited to join the LAUNCH Incubator by investor Jason Calicanis.

[Links]   Web: blanket.ai Twitter: @blanketai

acer
I AM BUILDING

Employees have a question or service request.
Spoke gives the right answer without any human intervention
Chang
Chang
Yup!
MacBook Pro

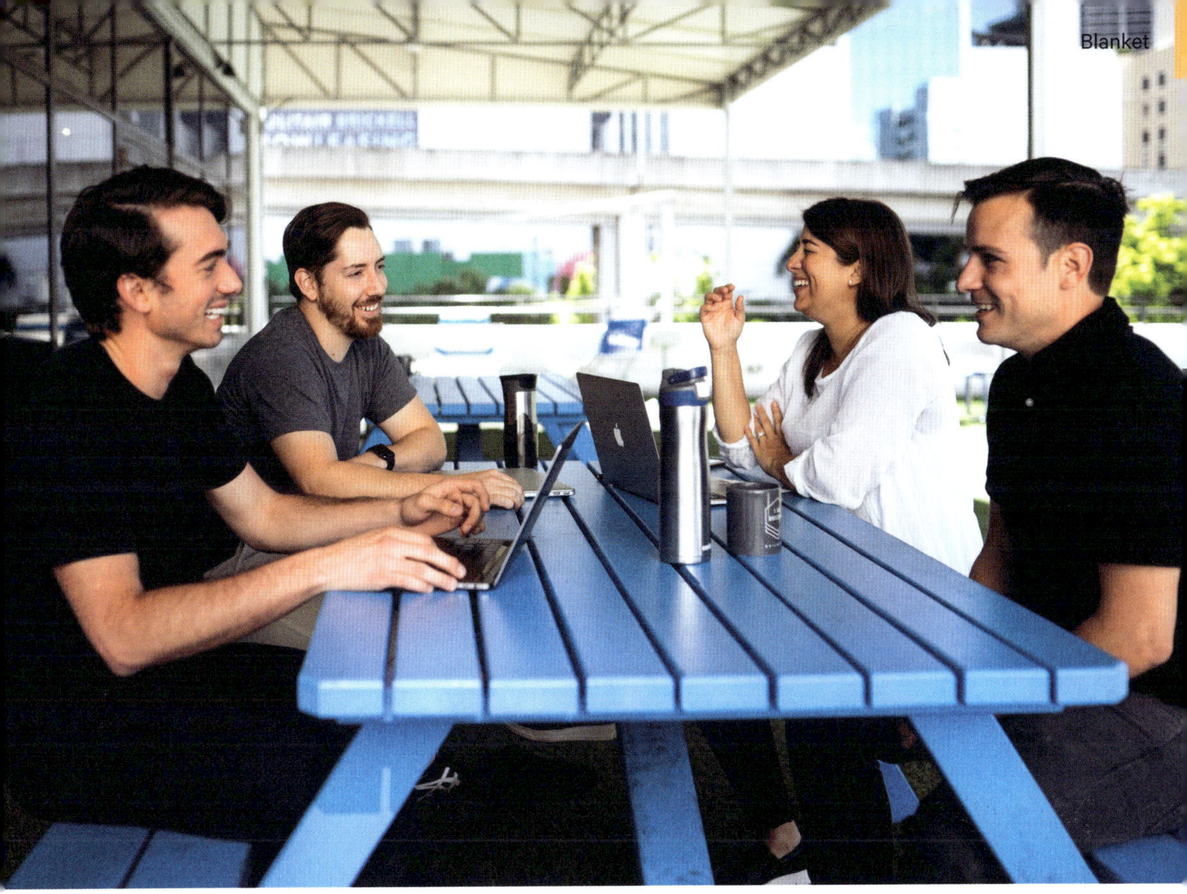

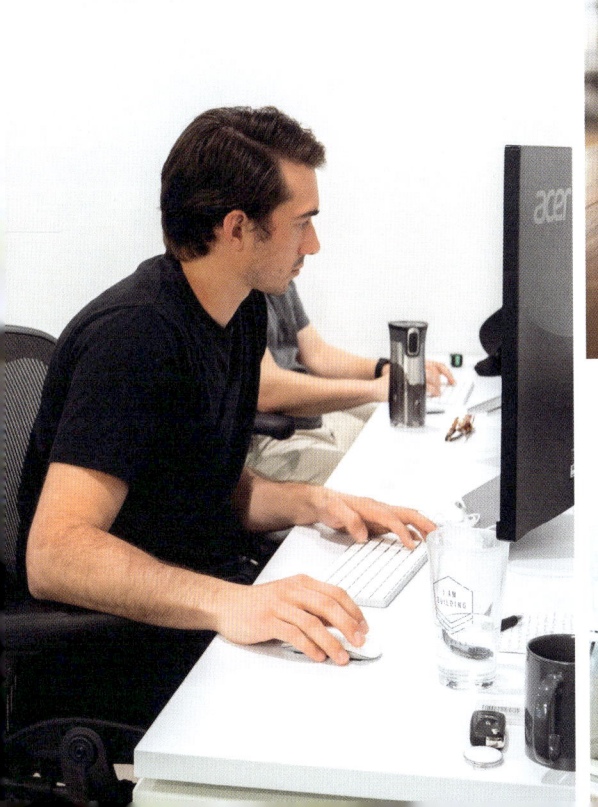

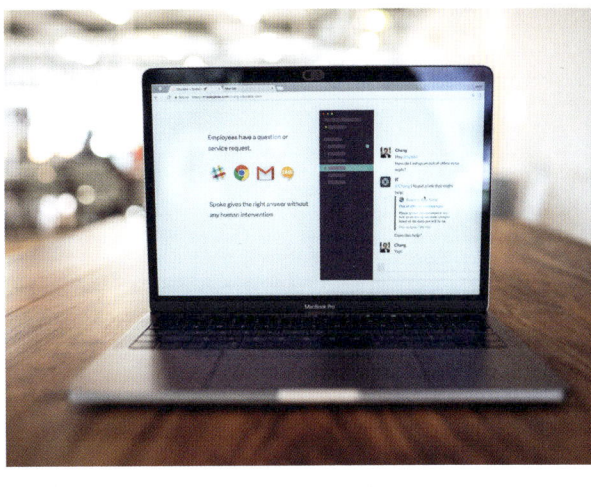

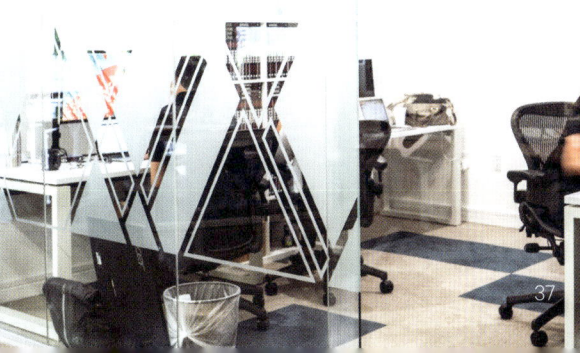

[Name] # CarePredict

[Elevator Pitch] *"We're an AI-powered elder-care platform that allows us to empower better senior care for folks living in assisted living facilities and aging at home. We do that by tracking activity and behavior patterns of seniors and understanding the precursors to declines in health."*

[The Story] Each time Satish Movva, founder and CEO of CarePredict, would visit his aging parents he was troubled to find new health conditions he hadn't been aware of that required immediate medical care. "It got to the point where I recognized I could no longer rely on one to keep the other safe, and I needed something objective," Satish says. But when he looked online for devices to help monitor their health, he found outdated, and even obsolete, technology such as motion-sensing. "The leap of faith the existing systems required was immense. Just because a refrigerator door opened and closed doesn't mean the person has had anything to eat."

Using his prior experience in the healthcare industry and the money raised during a successful exit, Satish began developing his own solution to this problem. His innovation, Tempo, is a wearable wrist-watch style device that uses advanced deep-learning algorithms to monitor elderly people's activity and behavior patterns for the changes that precede health issues, alerting friends and families of problems before they develop. The product couldn't be timelier. In as little as the next two decades, an estimated one in five people worldwide will be over the age of sixty-five. "Senior care has been underserved for a very long time," Satish says, "and we need to be looking for solutions to that today."

[Funding History]

Bootstrap   Angel   External

Initially, Satish bootstrapped CarePredict using money raised from the sale of a previous venture. Since then, the company has raised $10.2 million from venture capitalists and angel investors.

[Milestones]
- Successfully developing a deep-learning algorithm that accurately predicts an elder's health.
- Piloting product in assisted living facilities for sixteen months.
- Launching product in countries around the world, including Canada, Japan and Argentina in 2018.
- Signing commercial contracts with LifeWell, Crown, Avanti and Tradition Senior Living.

[Links] Web: **carepredict.com** Facebook: CarePredict Twitter: @CarePredict

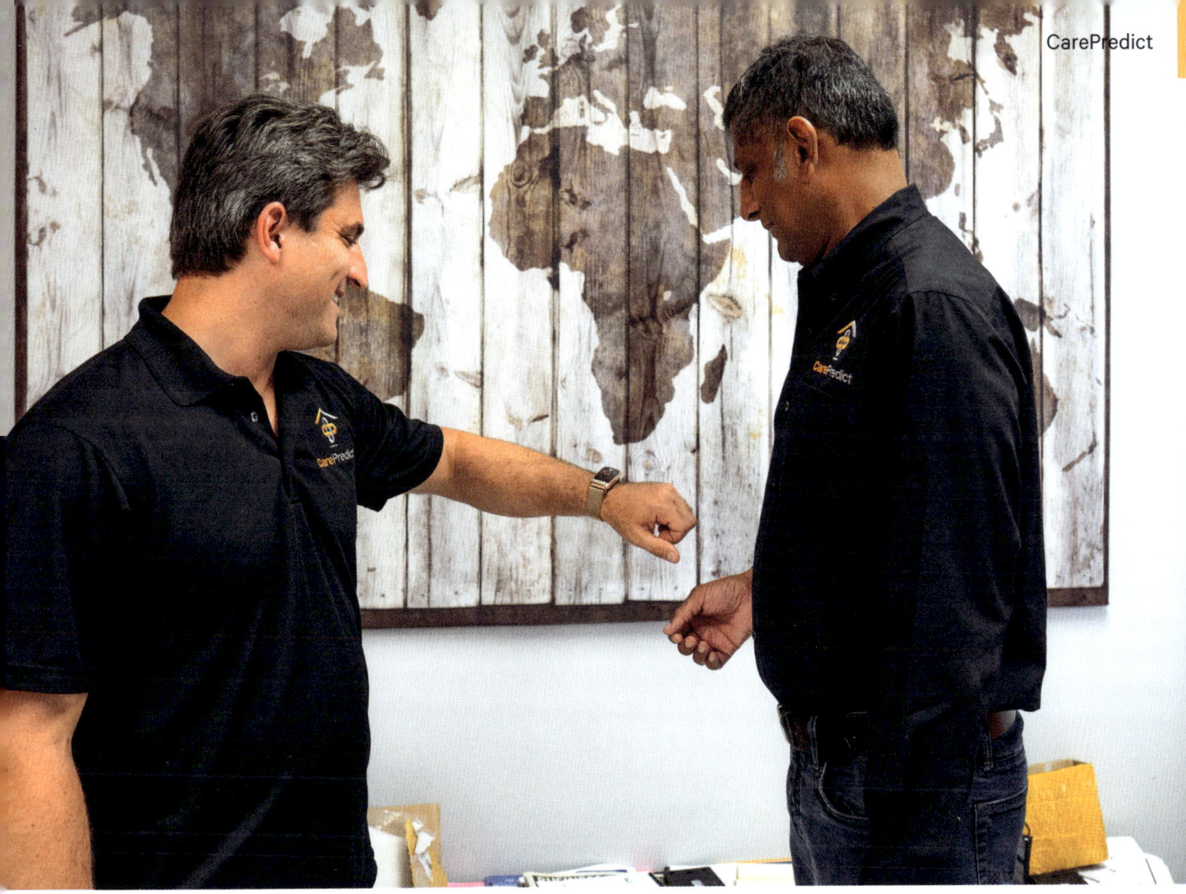

[Name]
Caribu

[Elevator Pitch]
"We're an education platform that helps parents, extended family and mentors to read and draw with children when they are not in the same location."

[The Story]
Alvaro Sabido was studying towards his MBA in innovation, entrepreneurship and management at Imperial College London when he saw a Facebook image of a soldier reading a storybook to his daughter via webcam. This inspired his class project: an interactive video app that allows users to see each other and the book they're reading. "This all started because I thought parents separated from their families should be able to do something as simple as read a bedtime story to their kids," Alvaro says. Caribu was made available in the Apple app store in 2014. It received a surprisingly high amount of organic growth, and was even featured in a keynote speech at an Apple event.

By 2016, Alvaro believed Caribu could be a business, and recruited Maxeme Tuchman as CEO. "I was extremely impressed by the organic growth," says Maxeme, who was previously director of Teach For America's Miami office and appointed to serve as a White House Fellow in the Treasury Department. "I knew we could work together and make something out of it." They moved the bootstrapped business to Miami and sustained it by participating in pitch competitions. Today, Caribu has over 200,000 downloads, with users in 148 different countries. It offers hundreds of preloaded books in six different languages. "The future is global domination," Maxeme says. "We want to bring every family separated by distance closer together."

[Funding History]

Bootstrap   Pre-Seed   Seed   Angel

Caribu initially bootstrapped and fundraised by participating in pitch competitions and reinvesting the prize money into the business. They raised $160,000 in preseed money in November of 2017, and another $1.3 million in seed investment in 2018.

[Milestones]
- Getting unexpected organic growth from the day we launched, which motivated us to build out the product.
- Being featured in an Apple keynote speech in 2014.
- Being featured in several iPad TV ads in 2015.
- Joining up with Maxeme Tuchman to launch the business in earnest.
- Maxeme Tuchman being named the 2018 Toyota Mother of Invention.
- Winning the 1776 Global Pitch Competition.

[Links]
Web: **caribu.com** Facebook: **Caribu** Twitter: **@caribu** Instagram: **caribu**

ChronWell

[Elevator Pitch]

"We're a company created to fix workers' compensation by building a great relationship with the injured worker using artificial intelligence and humans. As we evolve, we'll also become a technology-enabled claims processor and eventually disrupt the workers compensation market at all levels."

[The Story]

Initially, Joe Rubinsztain, cofounder and CEO of ChronWell, had no intention of disrupting the workers' compensation market. In fact, his initial goal was to develop a technology to address insuring individuals with chronic illnesses. He quickly found, however, that when he proposed technology solutions for the problem, he came up against pushback on the insurer level. "We discovered that insurers were not so interested in an automatic solution because people switch their insurance every eighteen months or so," Joe says. As they continued to research the insurance market, they discovered a $100 billion area that seemed to be operating "in the dark ages of technology." That area was workers' compensation, and it was from that discovery that ChronWell was born.

ChronWell was founded with the aim of using tech to humanize workers' comp. The company takes workers through the entire workers' compensation process through an easy-to-use platform. Throughout the process, case managers check in with the worker to ensure that they're getting the care and attention they deserve. "We stay in touch to see how you're doing. We're monitoring everything, and we're making sure that everybody is well coordinated and that the employee feels that the company cares about them," Joe says. "A little humanity in a system that's much more focused on process is something that's very welcome."

[Funding History]

Bootstrap

External

Joe Rubinsztain, along with cofounders Sam Rubinsztain and Salomon Sredni, initially bootstrapped ChronWell with money they had raised in a previous exit in the healthcare field. They then raised a $5 million Series A round in February of this year alongside investors who had invested in their previous company, as well as other investors who joined later.

[Milestones]
- Researching the product and building the team over the course of the first six months.
- Growing to a team of thirteen people, with more employees expected to be added soon.
- Launching our first pilot with an initial 5,000 employees, which will increase to 180,000 employees over the course of the pilot.
- Raising a Series A round in 2018.

[Links]   Web: chronwell.com Twitter: @ChronwellInc

ChronWell Recovry

[Name]
DeepBlocks

[Elevator Pitch]
"We leverage artificial intelligence to optimize real estate development."

[The Story]
DeepBlocks was founded on the belief that artificial intelligence can make real estate development less complicated by providing real-time analysis of financial and market data and local building regulations and using that to generate a set of optimal strategies for any project. Cofounders Olivia Ramos and Bernard Leong came up with the idea in 2016 while attending Singularity University, a Silicon Valley think tank and business incubator. They were studying strategies for using technology to solve the global housing issue. "I was explaining to Bernard all the different experts it takes to build a building, between architects, developers, brokers, contractors and appraisers," says Olivia, who has an MBA in architecture and real estate development. "Seeing those pain points, Bernard said, 'We should have an AI do this.' It was a simple thing to say, but it totally changed my world."

After graduating from the program in 2017, Bernard moved on to pursue other opportunities, and Olivia shifted the business to Miami, where real estate development is the number-one industry. DeepBlocks aims to simplify the build process, allowing more economic and efficient development. "An AI system can understand finance, architecture and design all at the same time," Olivia says. "As a real estate developer, that means you already have an idea of what would be optimal before you even do any work."

[Funding History]

Bootstrap   Seed   Angel   External

DeepBlocks fundraised while in the Singularity University incubator before receiving $1 million in seed money after moving into Singularity's accelerator in 2016. In 2017, DeepBlocks raised another $1.3 million in seed money from a combination of institutional investors, angel investors and real estate developers.

[Milestones]
- Being admitted into Singularity University in 2016.
- Finding top tech talent and convincing them to come to Miami to help build DeepBlocks.
- Visiting Beijing to learn how to build an international version of our product (planned for 2019).
- Getting real estate developers (typically brick-and-mortar investors) to invest in our seed round.

[Links]   Web: deepblocks.com Facebook: DeepBlocksAI Twitter: @deepblocks

[Name]
Home61

[Elevator Pitch]

"We're a technology-powered real estate agency that reduces the inefficiencies experienced by renters, buyers and real estate agents. The backend technology enables scheduling of showings and on-demand access to agents, analytics and notes."

[The Story]

Olivier Grinda, CEO and cofounder of Home61, got the idea for his company after moving to Miami from Brazil in early 2013. He'd already built a couple of successful companies in the Latin American ecommerce market and was excited to invest in a new sector: real estate. But when he began to take the first steps toward buying a home, he was sorely disappointed. "I thought having a place you can see and feel and touch would be really cool," he says. "Then I started the process, and it was horrible. I'm still pissed off to this day." The deeper he dug into the process of home-buying, the more frustrating he found it. Everything from the initial search to signing legal documents after the sale was riddled with inefficiencies, hidden fees and other hassles.

Sensing that no one out there was solving the problem, Olivier did what many entrepreneurs do: he built the solution himself. The result, Home61, is a data-enabled software platform that takes homebuyers through the entire process. It connects them with qualified agents who speak their language and know the market, finds the right home using advanced geolocalization tools, and streamlines paperwork when they decide to make an offer. "It's all based on data," Olivier says. "We're able to create a very different experience for the largest investment in people's lives: their homes."

[Funding History]

Bootstrap   Seed   Angel   External

After successful exits in previous companies, Olivier Grinda raised his first round of capital organically with help from friends and family. In 2017, Home61 raised a $4 million seed round led by FF Angel, which is run by Peter Thiel's venture capital firm Founders Fund. Olivier plans to use that money to expand to other cities.

[Milestones]

- Completing the first deal that came through the website.
- Introducing "Teddy," the small teddy bear that welcomes all Home61 clients into their new homes.
- Being covered in Tech Crunch after raising a $4 million seed round through FF Angel.
- Closing more than one thousand deals in Miami, and preparing to announce a second city in the coming months.

[Links]   Web: home61.com   Facebook: home61   Twitter: @home61exp   Instagram: home61experience

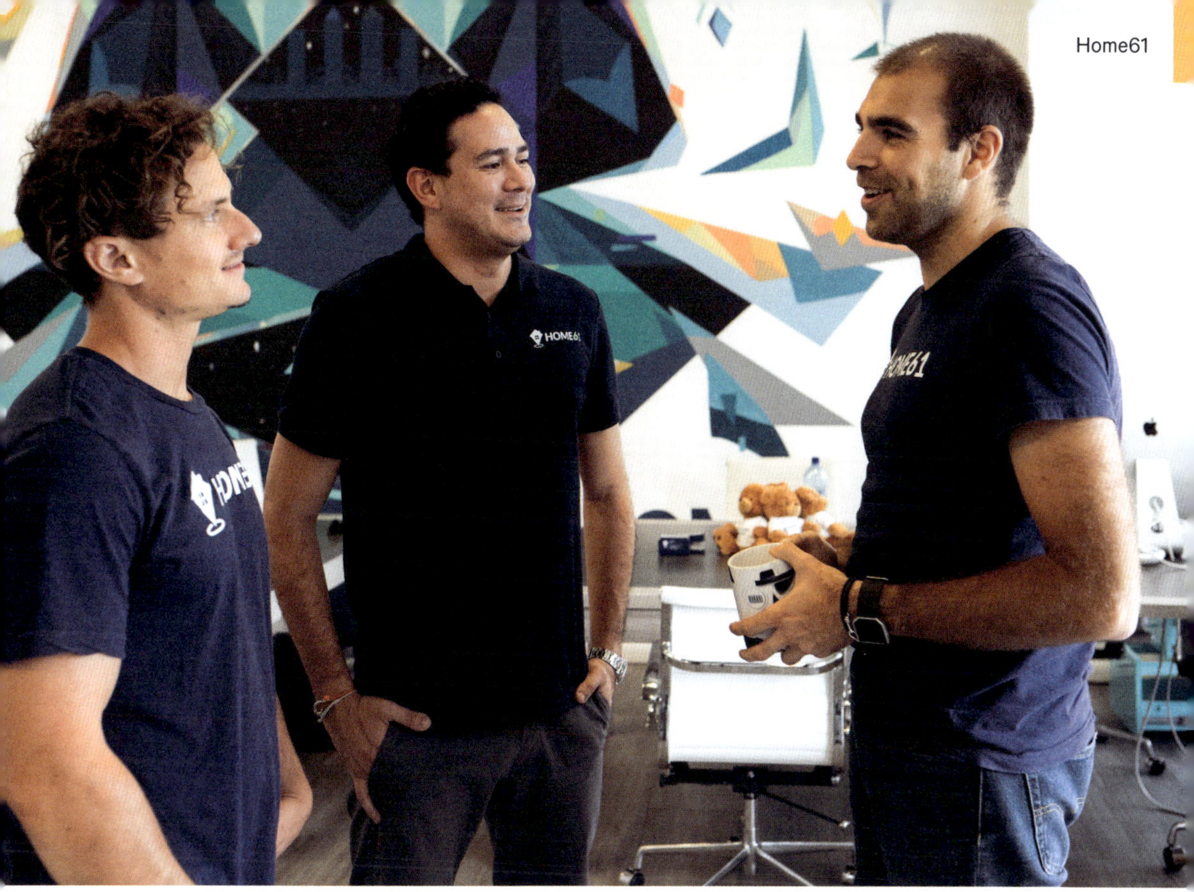
HOME61

HOME61
HAPPY CLIENTS WALL
GLASS OF SUCCESS
SOLD

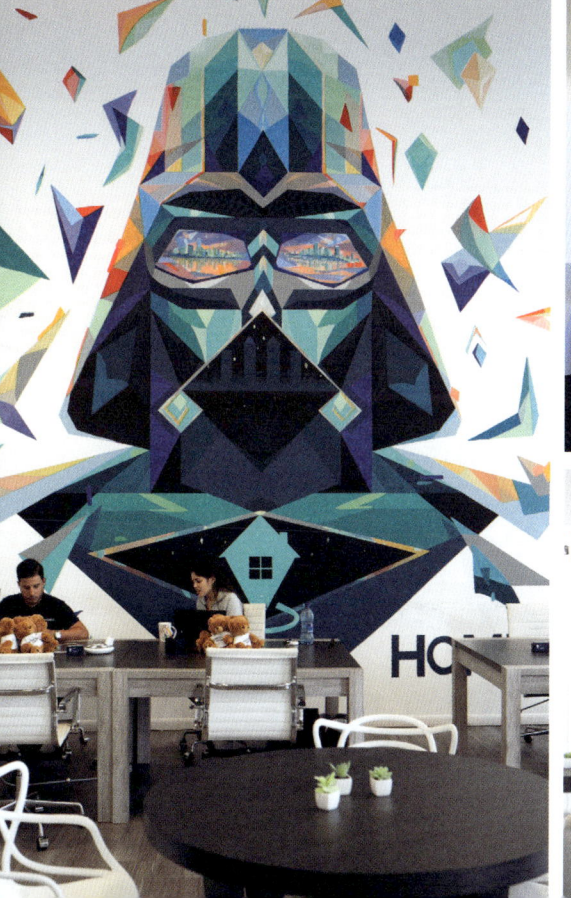

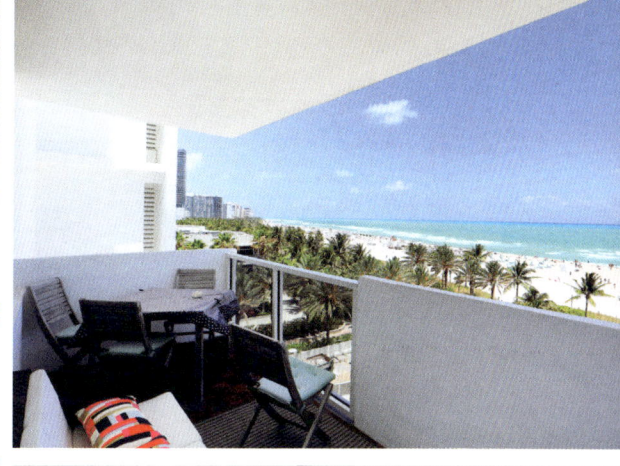

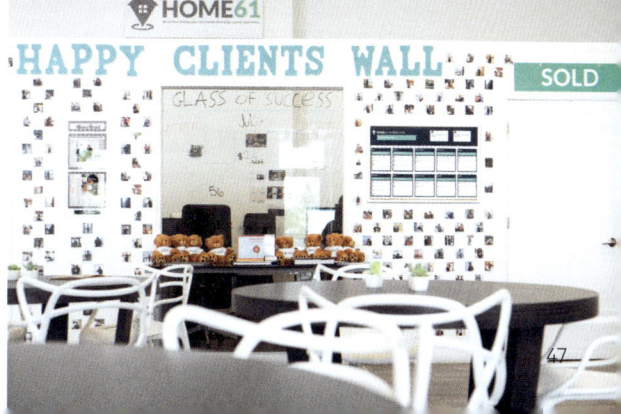

[Name]
Magic Leap

[Elevator Pitch]
"We are a company made up of hundreds of artists, engineers, explorers and dreamers from around the globe, all chasing their curiosity toward the same goal: bringing together the digital and real worlds to advance human potential."

[The Story]
Since he was a kid, Magic Leap founder and CEO Rony Abovitz loved getting up close and personal with nature. From snorkeling with tropical fish to chasing fireflies, he found inspiration in the natural world. But Rony felt that for admirers of nature like himself, gaming and immersive technology failed to replicate the real world. "I realized what the real world could give in abundance, our past and current technologies lacked: visceral experience, " he wrote in a 2014 blog post. "Magic Leap was founded on an idea: that computing and technology should bend to us, to our needs, to our humanity and to our experience."

Magic Leap is Rony's attempt to do just that. Founded in 2011, Magic Leap is a new kind of immersive experience called "spatial computing" that can project digital objects into the physical world through a wearable device and have the two interact with one another. With Magic Leap, users can pet dragons, interact with underwater creatures and fight robots from the comfort of their living room – without feeling like they're in a simulation. For Rony and his team, turning Magic Leap into a reality was years in the making. The hermetic company publicly launched in 2014, but eager gamers and techbuffs had to wait four years before the launch of Magic Leap One, a new device fully realizing Magic Leap's technology. Now the possibilities are endless.

[Funding History]

Bootstrap

External

For its first three years, Magic Leap was funded from the $1.6 billion sale of Rony's previous company, Mako Surgical Corp. According to Crunchbase, since then Magic Leap has raised an estimated $2.3 billion across multiple rounds from investors including Google, Alibaba and Saudi Arabia's Public Investment Fund.

[Milestones]
- Launching Magic Leap One Creator Edition in August 2018.
- Partnering with German company Brainlab to develop tech-enabled medical imaging and surgical procedures.
- Opening our first international optics and photonics center in Lausanne, Switzerland.
- Holding the L.E.A.P conference and bringing together creators working on spatial computing.

[Links]   Web: magicleap.com Facebook: magicleap Twitter: @magicleap Instagram: magicleap

[Name]

Octopi

[Elevator Pitch]

"We're a software service for cargo port terminals. We help them digitize their operations so they can see what's happening at the port in real time and improve their performance by tracking key performance indicators."

[The Story]

Luc Castera, founder of Octopi, had a wealth of experience in the software industry when a friend came to him with a challenge: his friend, whose family had operated a small port terminal for three generations, was looking to modernize the software used at his port. When Luc looked at the software options available online, he made a startling discovery. "I started to realize that it's an industry that's living thirty years in the past when it comes to software and that there was a huge market opportunity there," he says. "That's when we decided to bite the bullet, seize the opportunity and build software for ports."

The result is Octopi, a web-based operating system for seaport cargo terminals. Whereas before port operators balanced logistics with their two hands, Octopi gives them eight. Through the software platform, companies can manage intake, track shipments, communicate with partners and visualize productivity data in real time. The company now serves seven customers in five countries: the US, Haiti, Barbados, Brazil and Madagascar. Being based out of Miami, a major shipping hub in the Caribbean and to some the unofficial capital of Latin America, gives Octopi a competitive advantage. "We're located in a global city, and we're serving a global consumer base," Luc says. "Every time we sign a new port, we learn so much about their country, their culture and their economy."

[Funding History]

Bootstrap

Octopi signed on its first client before it was even officially a company, helping Luc Castera and his cofounder Guille Carlos to bootstrap funding for technology development and the team. It has since increased its revenue by closing deals and adding new customers. The company has not raised outside investment.

[Milestones]

- Signing our first customer and launching the company in October 2015.
- Reaching a five-year agreement with Haiti's Caribbean Port Services and bringing in significant revenue.
- Winning eMerge Americas 2016 Startup Showcase competition.
- Adding our first customer outside of the Americas in Madagascar.

[Links]   Web: octopi.co Facebook: octopitos Twitter: @octopi_tos

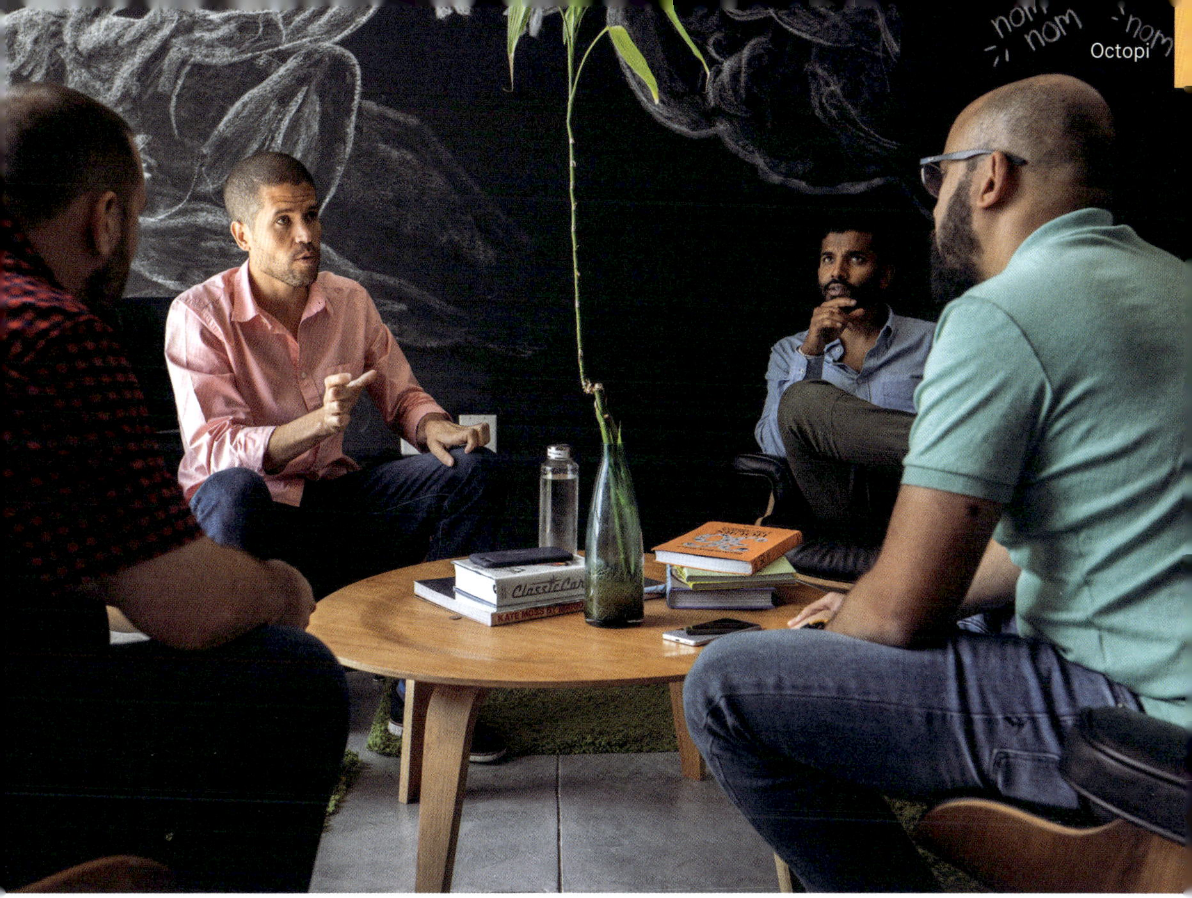
nom
nom
nom

CORE VALUES
Respect
Data Driven
Fearless
Quality
Focus
Curiosity

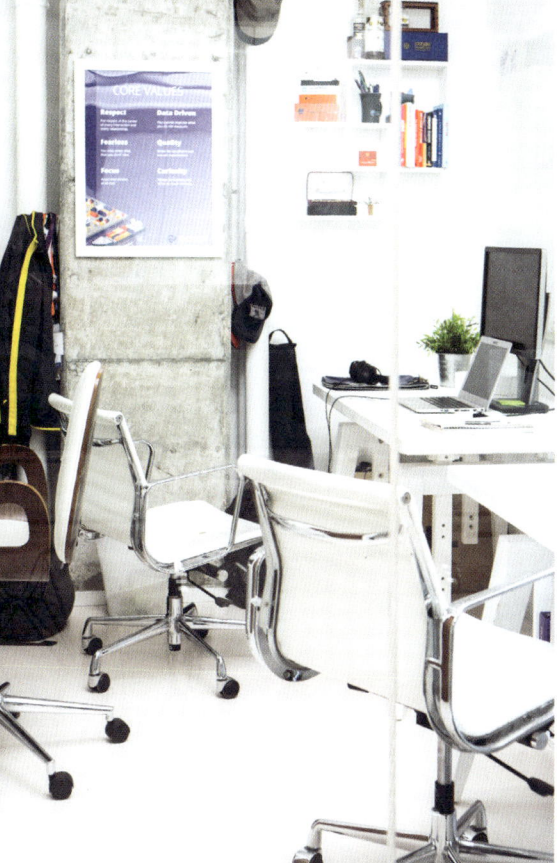

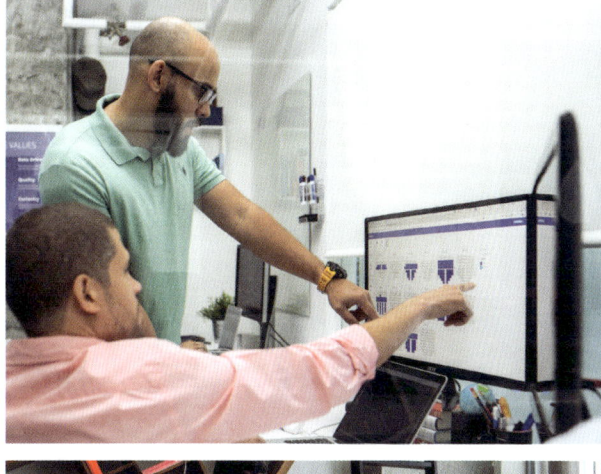

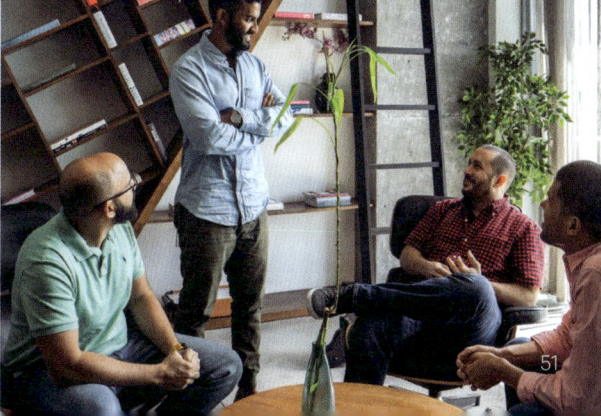

[Name]
Plum

[Elevator Pitch]
"Plum is the first fully automatic wine appliance that identifies, chills, preserves and serves any two bottles of wine by the glass."

[The Story]
Like many great inventions, Plum was born out of a frustration with existing technologies. In 2014, Plum founder and wine lover David Koretz saw a glaring gap in two experiences that could – and, he believed, should – be quite similar: enjoying the perfect cup of coffee in the morning, and enjoying a perfect glass of wine at night. David wanted to be able to pour a single glass of wine with the touch of a button, much like he did with his Jura, and without having to worry about diminishing the quality of the wine by uncorking it. But when he perused the market, he didn't find any devices that could do that. So he set out to build his own. "We wanted to create a way to enjoy wine in a manner that meets the way we live today – an on-demand lifestyle," says Stephanie Faskow, director of marketing and customer acquisition at Plum.

Plum, a sleek countertop appliance that fits up to two wine bottles at a time, and chills, pours, and preserves wine for up to ninety days without ever removing the cork. Fitted with internal cameras and wifi, Plum can recognize 6 million wines and keep those bottles at the right temperature until the bottle is finished, and no sooner.

[Funding History]

Angel

External

Plum has gone through multiple external investment rounds, including two Series A rounds led by Khosla Ventures for $5 million and $4 million, respectively, and more recently a $10 million Series B round led by Las Olas Venture Capital in May of 2018. The company also has partnerships with more than thirty-five hotels, and sells Plum to consumers for $1,999.

[Milestones]
- Founding Plum in 2015 and shipping our first products in 2017.
- Securing over thirty luxury hotel deals, with another fifteen expected in 2018.
- Launching a successful pre-order campaign, selling out initial inventory before shipping.
- Establishing retail partnerships with Williams Sonoma, Wine Enthusiast and local high-end appliance retailers.

[Links] Web: plum.wine Facebook: PlumAppliance Twitter: @WeArePlum Instagram: plum.wine

CHAPPELLET
2014
Napa Valley
Cabernet Sauvignon

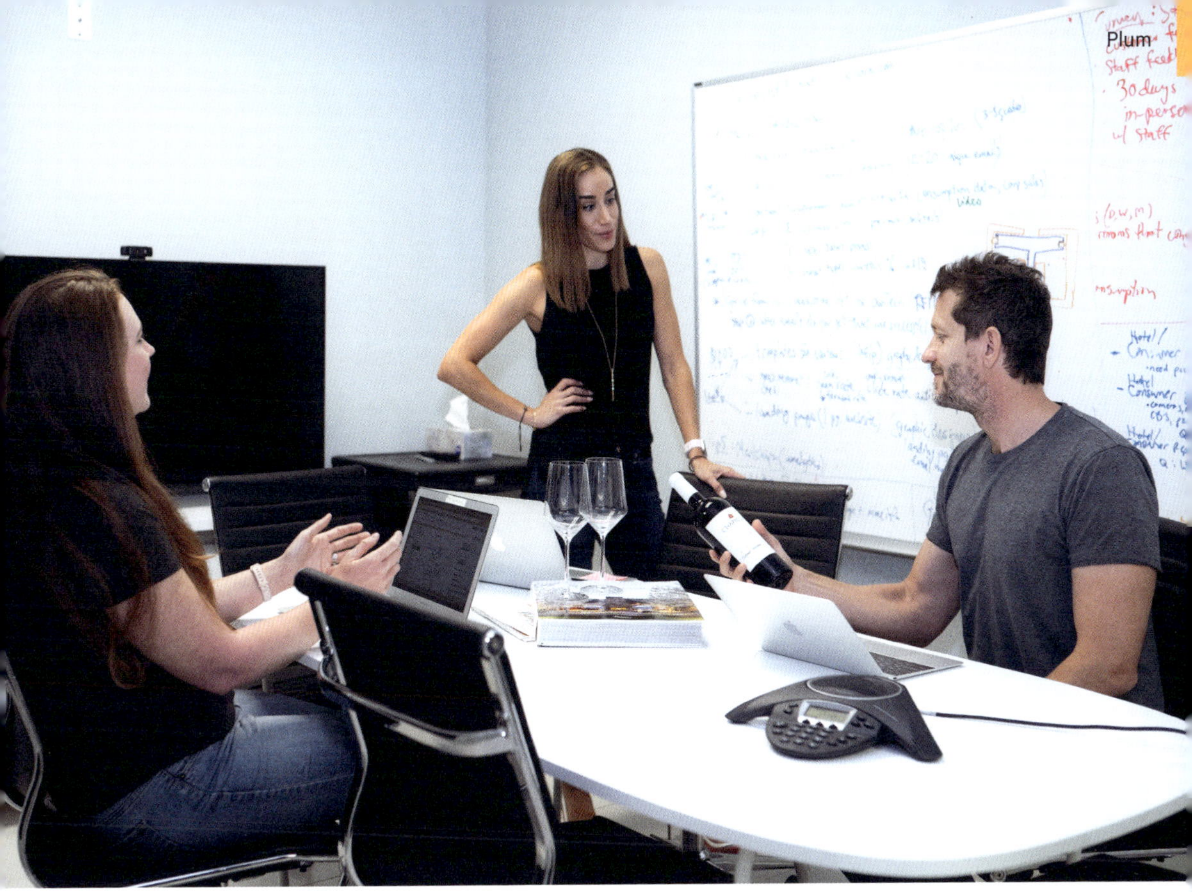

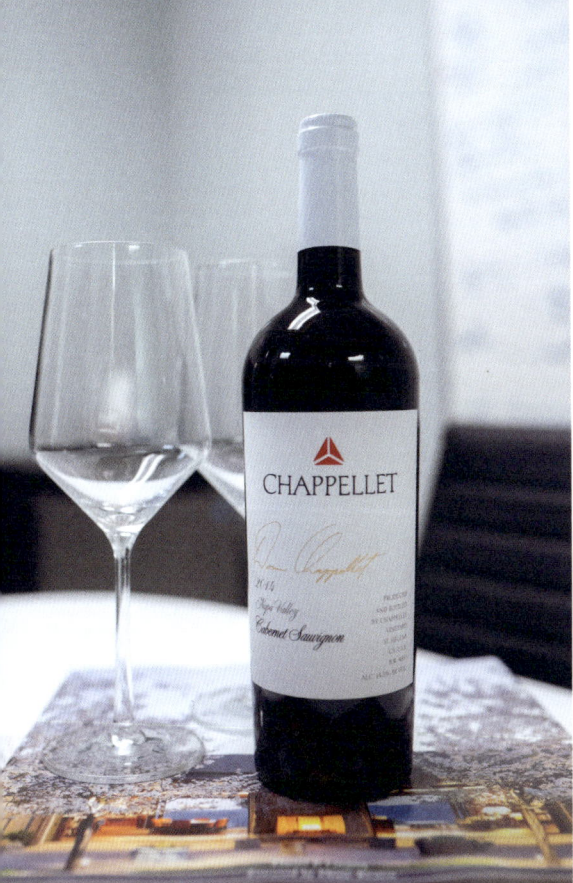

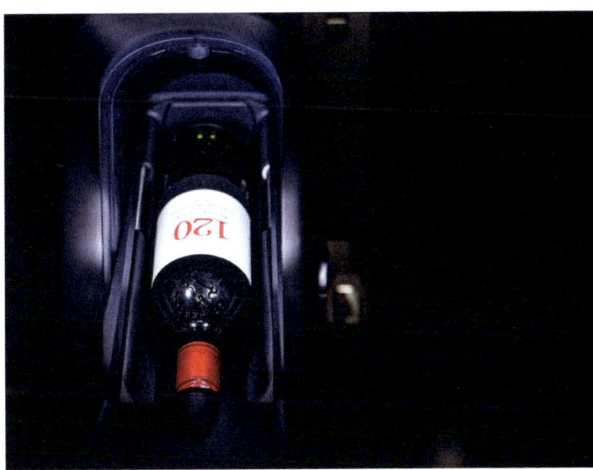

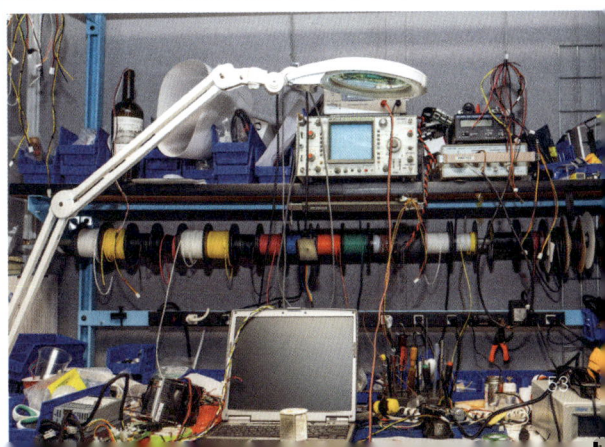

[Name]
SheWorks!

[Elevator Pitch]

"We're a platform with the goal of disrupting gender discrimination in employment and helping women access jobs that can be done flexibly and remotely."

[The Story]

In our interconnected world, working out of a traditional office is becoming a thing of the past. For women especially, a more flexible and remote work schedule can make a huge difference for maintaining a healthy work/life balance, increasing productivity and developing their careers. Yet many companies are still reluctant to hire remote female workers. SheWorks! helps employers and female employees work together better. "Having no flexibility and working in the old traditional models is not only obsolete, it doesn't make any sense: not for the women and not for the companies that want to hire them," says Silvina Moschini, CEO and founder of SheWorks! "I'm a woman, I saw a need and I'm passionate about technology, so I decided to do something about it."

Through a two-way talent exchange and a remote-workers management platform, SheWorks! connects employers to qualified female employees using machine learning and matching algorithms, and manages that professional relationship through an online collaboration platform. SheWorks! has also partnered with Ernst & Young and the W20 to provide free job training to women around the world through the SheWorks! Academy. The goal is to train and employ at least one hundred thousand women in the next five years. "If we get a couple of countries using our technology platform to create national employment programs," says Silvina, "one hundred thousand is just one country or less."

[Funding History]

Bootstrap

External

Through a combination of $3 million in self-funding, external investment from individual donors and corporate partnerships, SheWorks! bypassed the need for venture capital. In addition, SheWorks! provides company equity in exchange for services, including advertising and consulting.

[Milestones]
- Launching and managing remote company with no offices and talent in more than twenty-five countries.
- Securing partnerships with Facebook, Google, Microsoft, SAP, Cisco and Ernst & Young.
- Bringing on board a former president, a journalist, a former CEO and a company president.
- Meeting with Facebook cofounder and CEO Mark Zuckerberg at Facebook F8 conference.
- Being named finalist for Tech Awards Leadership Category at 2018 FQUALS conference.

[Links]   Web: wheresheworks.com Facebook: SheWorksCloud Twitter: @SheWorksCloud

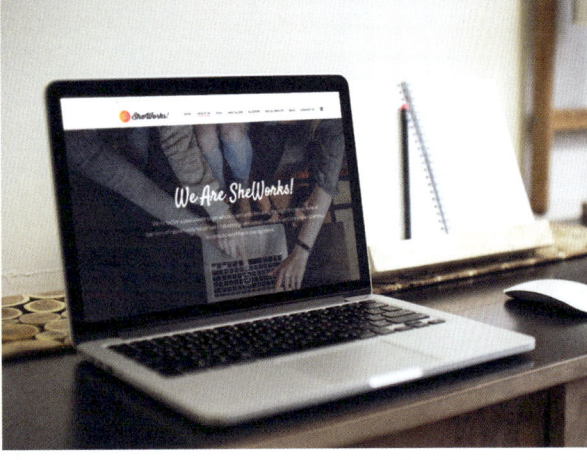

[Name] # Voyhoy

[Elevator Pitch] *"We're a multi-modal travel platform where you can compare and purchase bus, flight, train, ferry and rideshare throughout South America at affordable prices."*

[The Story] Voyhoy was started by three friends who wanted to make traveling around South America easier. While living in Santiago, Chile, Jake Moskowitz, Roger Robinson and Ignacio Vial experienced firsthand the frustrations of travelling around the region. "The digital travel infrastructure was extremely fragmented," says Jake, who was working for a group travel agency at the time. "It was impossible to book intercity travel online." The trio came up with the idea to consolidate the entire travel-booking experience in one platform, but before they could sign up travel operators, they had to validate demand. "We started just by scraping websites for bus, train and airline prices and schedules," Jake says. "This at least gave people the opportunity to compare costs."

Traffic to the site quickly grew, and they began signing up travel vendors all over Chile. The commercial version of Voyhoy, with travel tickets available to purchase, launched in 2015. Today, it has sold over 100,000 tickets, and 80 percent of travel operators in Chile, Colombia, Peru and Argentina sell travel on Voyhoy. Now headquartered out of Miami with a second office in Santiago, Voyhoy recently launched a "smart ticket" system, allowing travelers to book multiple legs of travel on one ticket. It has plans to expand into Brazil, Ecuador and Bolivia. "Our goal is to connect all of South and Latin America," Jake says.

[Funding History]

Bootstrap   Pre-Seed   Seed   Angel

Voyhoy was initially bootstrapped before raising funds from Chilean angel investors to grow the team and product. In 2016 Voyhoy received pre-seed funding from Techstars, and then closed a seed round from institutional investors in 2017 to fuel expansion and growth. Voyhoy is currently raising a Series A.

[Milestones]
- Launching a monetized version of our product.
- Validating multi-model platform by providing options for different types of travel.
- Becoming the first Chilean company accepted into Techstars accelerator program.
- Moving to Miami, the nexus between the US and Latin America.
- Hiring our marketing director from Skyscanner.
- Launching in Argentina, Peru and Colombia.

[Links] Web: voyhoy.com/en Facebook: yovoyhoy Twitter: @voyhoy Instagram: voyhoy

Voyhoy
Save time and money

MARCH
FOR OUR
LIVES

TRAVEL SMART WITH VOYHOY
MacBook Air

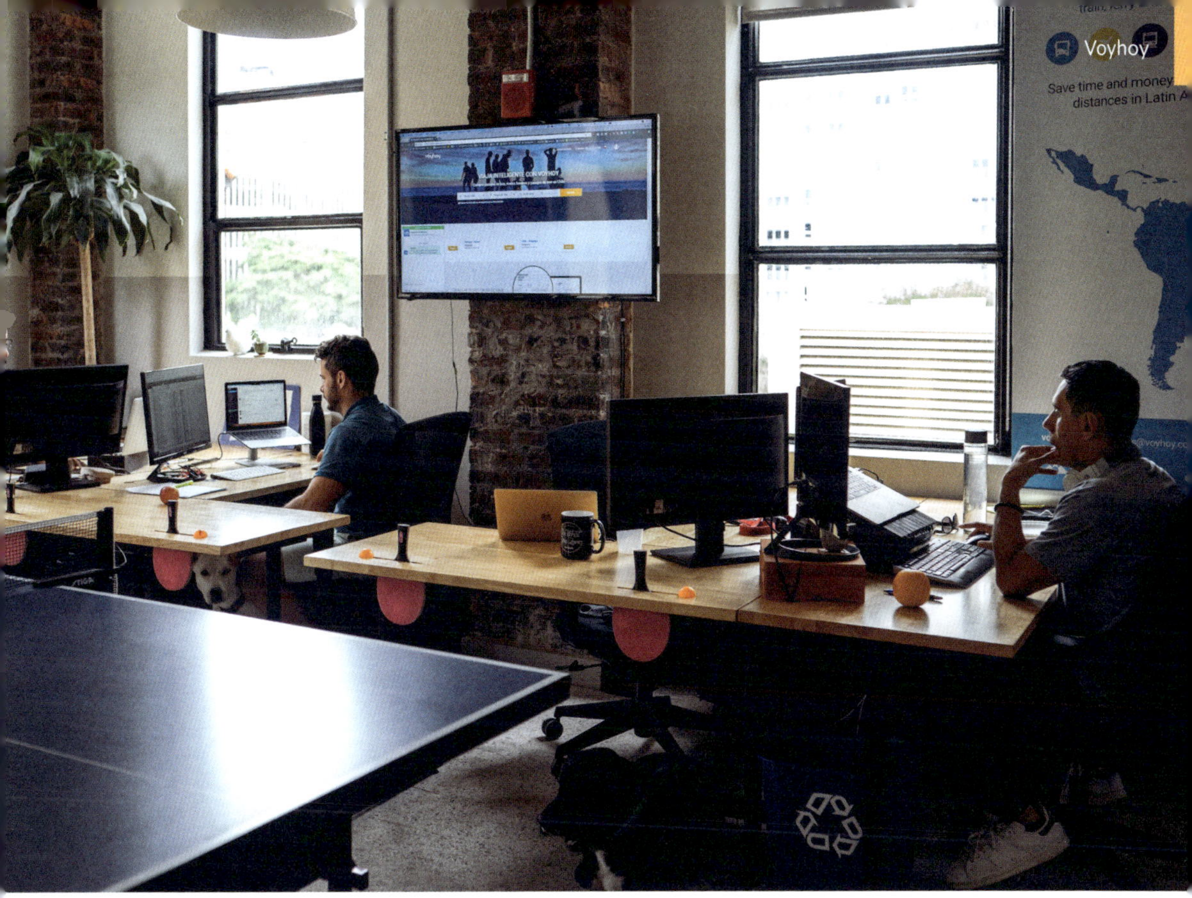

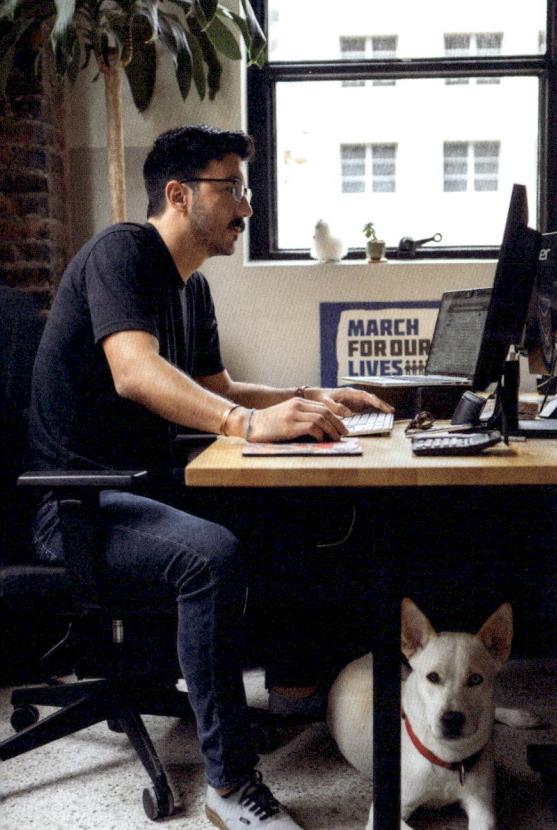

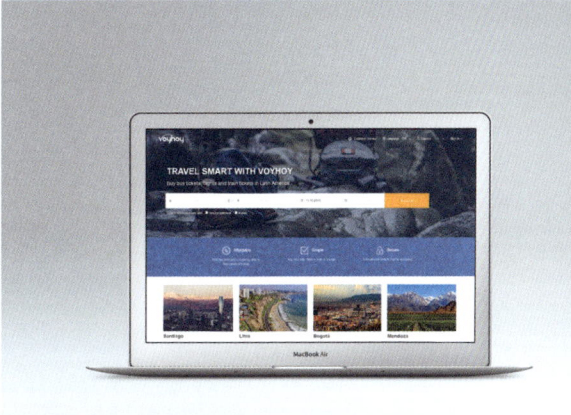

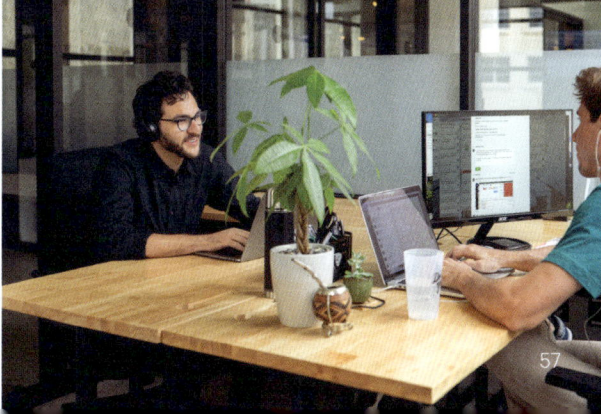

[Name]

Xendoo

[Elevator Pitch]

"We're a cloud-based monthly subscription service providing bookkeeping and accounting services for small business owners with fewer than twenty employees."

[The Story]

For small business owners, crunching numbers can be a painful task, especially when you have no other option but to go it alone. Lillian Roberts, cofounder of Xendoo, knows this firsthand. A self-described "serial entrepreneur," Lillian has founded and served as a shareholder for several companies, and in doing so has always butted up against this same issue. "In all my years of owning businesses and building businesses, certified public accounting was the most painful point of the business because you could never get your numbers when you needed them," she says. "Accounting is an industry that doesn't take care of small business owners."

Along with her cofounder Steven Gelley, Lillian set out to disrupt the accounting industry for small businesses. The result, Xendoo, is a cloud-based service that takes small business owners through the entire life-cycle of a company's finances, from monthly bookkeeping to filing taxes at the end of the year. Xendoo works with clients across a number of spaces, including ecommerce, hospitality, retail services, medical services and professional services such as IT, marketing and web design. The company aims to reach sixty thousand users in the next five years. "The space is starting to heat up, and we're one of the early movers," Lillian says. "We want to reshape an industry."

[Funding History]

Bootstrap   Seed

Xendoo was initially self-funded as Lillian and her team worked to develop the software and de-risk the model. They brought on initial users at trade shows, which allowed them to further de-risk the model and appeal to investors. The company closed its first seed round in Q4 of 2017.

[Milestones]

- Launching our first product in August of 2017, around nine months after being founded.
- Being featured in the premiere episode of CNBC's The Job Interview.
- Bringing on a full team of sixteen people.
- Winning the 2018 eMerge Americas' Startup Showcase competition, and being invited into investor Jason Calicanis' LAUNCH Incubator.

[Links]   Web: xendoo.com Facebook: xendoo Twitter: @Xendoo_ Instagram: XendooAccounting

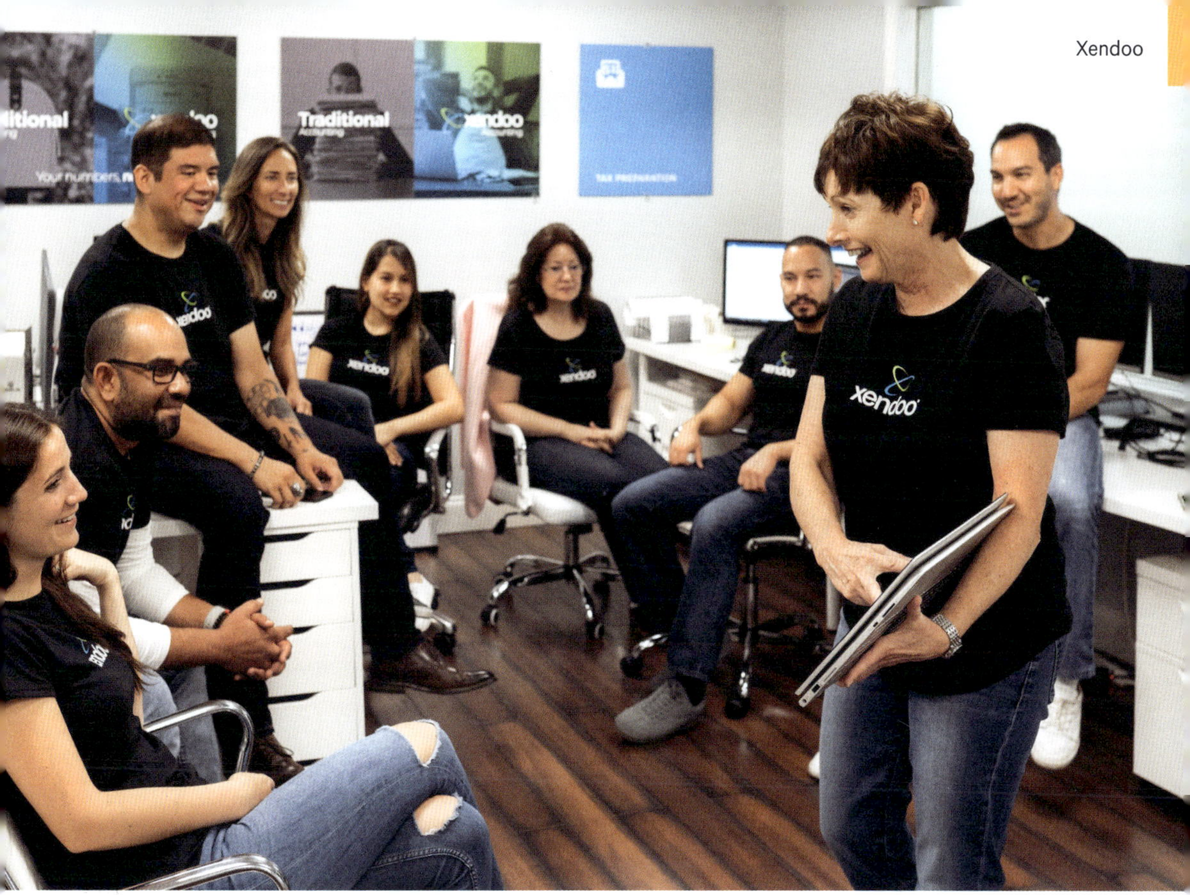
Traditional
xendoo
xendoo

xendoo
xendoo
Hawk Mountain
Sanctuary

36
58
34

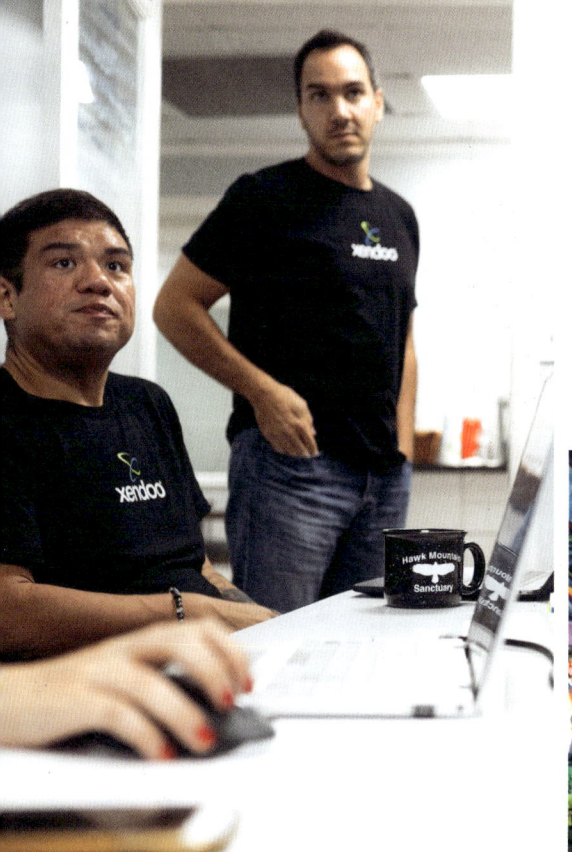

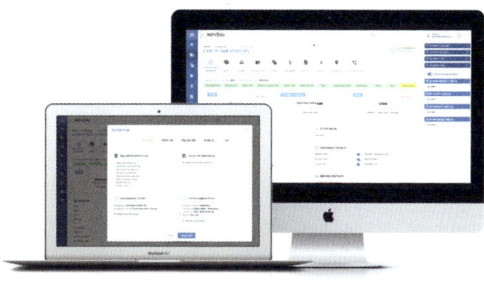

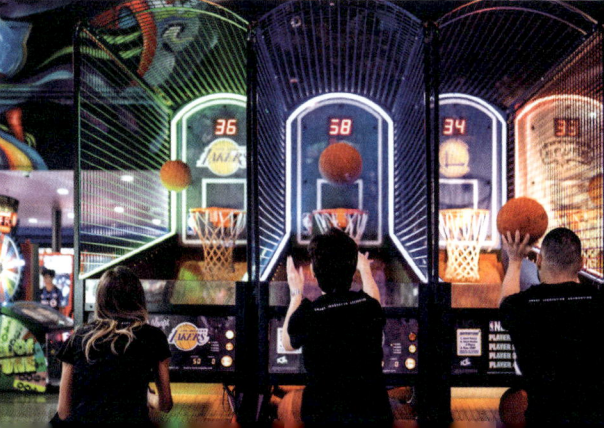

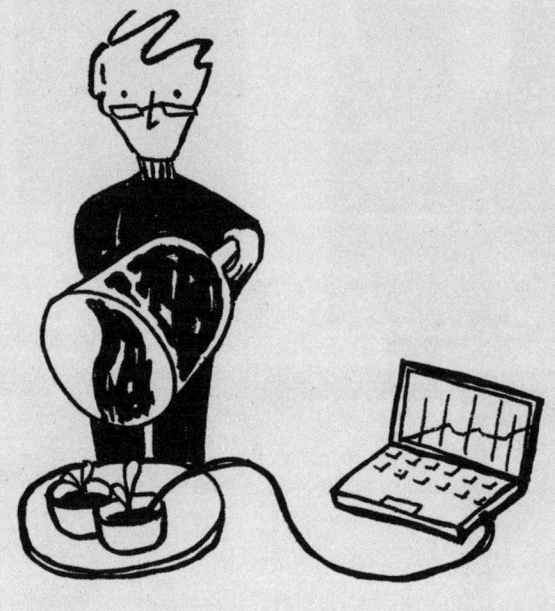

rams

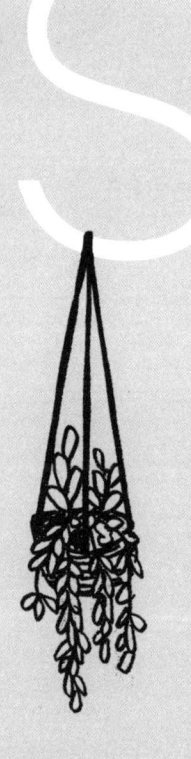

- **Have a great team.**
  Your team should have worked together successfully in the past and be open to coaching. You should be able to explain why your team is best suited to build and scale this business.

- **Have deep insight into your market.**
  You should offer experience, connections and a deep understanding of the sector you're seeking to disrupt.

- **Have great products that will disrupt large and/or growing markets.**
  Are you targeting a large and/or growing market? Have you achieved product-market fit, or are you likely to find it soon? Why will your product win the market over?

- **Show you have traction.**
  How many clients or users are actively using your product? Are they paying for it? How quickly are you growing?

[Name]

500 Startups

[Elevator Pitch]

"Our mission is to discover and back the world's most talented entrepreneurs, help them create successful companies at scale and build thriving global ecosystems."

[Sector]

Industry agnostic

[Description]

500 Startups is a venture capital fund and startup accelerator that invests in early-stage startups around the world. The fund started in Silicon Valley in 2010 and has grown to invest in over two thousand startups in over sixty countries. The Miami office, outfitted with coworking, training and event spaces, opened in April 2018 to capitalize on the city's growing startup ecosystem. "We believe Miami has the potential to be a global tech hub because of its geographic conditions, connectedness and diversity of its talent," says Ana Paula González, who leads 500 Startups Miami.

500 Startups typically invests in companies between pre-seed and Series A stages and strives to support talent that wouldn't otherwise have received an opportunity to access capital and mentorship. Most of its investments range from $50,000 to $250,000. "We make lots of little bets in different companies as a way to diversify risk and increase the probability of success," Ana says. "Through our accelerator program, we see which companies have greater potential and invest further." In Miami, 500 Startups has launched an ecosystem-development operation that supports founders, investors, corporates and the overall tech and innovation community. Programming includes free two-day founder bootcamps, accelerator programs for seed and Series A stage companies, investor seminars, corporate startup innovation-training sessions, demo days, speaker events and more.

To date, 500 Startups has invested in over twenty startups that are based in South Florida or have participated in South Florida programs. Ana hopes to leverage the 500 Startups global platform to continue supporting local founders, improve the quality of the local startups, and help them access resources and increase economic development in the region. "After working with over two thousand startups, we really know and understand what makes the difference in a team and a startup that will scale," Ana says. "We've built a brand over the past eight years by demonstrating we can help startups reach that inflection point."

[Apply to]

miami.500.co/miami

[Links]

Web: miami.500.co/miami Facebook: 500startups Twitter: @500Startups Instagram: 500startups

- **Be a passionate entrepreneur.**
  You need passion to be committed to building
  a scalable venture.

- **Think big.**
  We're looking for products and services that solve
  a big problem, have strong market positions and can
  easily scale.

- **Have a working prototype.**
  The resources we offer are best suited for companies
  that are past the ideation phase and have a prototype
  or market viable product.

- **Be an entrepreneur who can give back.**
  You should be willing to give back as much as you
  take from this program by engaging with other
  members and celebrating each other.

- **Apply in the spring.**
  Each year, we make applications for the upcoming
  start date available in the spring, typically during
  the middle or the end of March.

[Name]

Babson WIN Lab

[Elevator Pitch]

"We provide women entrepreneurs with an inspiring community and a rigorous, experiential process that catalyzes innovative thinking and enables them to successfully launch or transform businesses."

[Sector]

Women-focused venture accelerator

[Description]

Event planner Nathalie Cadet-Jones came to the Women Innovating Now (WIN) Lab at Babson College with an idea for a box that contains all the necessary items to host a successful dinner party. She left with thousands of dollars in revenue and three employees, and her business, *Luxe Fete*, won the Miami Herald's Business Plan Challenge. This is one of the success stories of the WIN Lab, an accelerator program designed specifically for women entrepreneurs. "We understand that women face different challenges when it comes to scaling startups, and by addressing them specifically we can get that much closer to achieving gender parity in the entrepreneurial ecosystem," says Michelle Abbs, director of the WIN Lab in Miami.

The WIN Lab at Babson College, ranked number one in the world by *U.S. News and World Report* for entrepreneurship education, was created in 2011 to address a lack of female founder participation both on the Babson campus and in larger accelerators nationally. The original WIN Lab was created on Babson's Wellesley campus and later relocated to the new downtown campus. A second WIN Lab opened on Babson's satellite campus in Miami in 2016 as a way to empower female founders in South Florida's emerging entrepreneurial ecosystem.

With support from Knight Foundation, the Miami WIN Lab offers five months of entrepreneurial programming to each year's applicant class tailored to provide a comprehensive leadership toolkit and framed by cutting-edge research on gender and leadership. "We're designed specifically for early-stage women entrepreneurs who want to accelerate their entrepreneurial paths and scale their businesses," Michelle says. "We're looking for women who want to disrupt, experiment and build successful startups on their own terms." The programming is valued at $25,000, Michelle says, but is free for the entrepreneurs accepted into each class. Miami's WIN Lab has graduated forty-four entrepreneurs in its first two years and has helped generate over $9 million in funding for their businesses.

[Apply to]

thewinlab.org/apply (applications reopen spring 2019)

[Links]

Web: thewinlab.org/miamiwinlab Facebook: thewinlab Twitter: @BabsonWIN

- **Have big, innovative ideas.**
  We want entrepreneurs with vision as well as
  leadership potential to inspire and lead companies
  to scale.

- **Be prepared to give back.**
  You should be willing to share your knowledge
  and financial gains with the next generation
  of entrepreneurs.

- **Believe in the Endeavor Mission**
  You should see the unique value in the Endeavor
  array of services.

- **Have a business model with traction.**
  Companies should be able to prove their business
  model can scale and create more wealth and jobs.

- **Show you're at the right stage.**
  We want to catch businesses at the right time.
  Entrepreneurs should be able to demonstrate that
  they're at an inflection point and that with Endeavor
  resources they can scale.

[Name] # Endeavor Miami

[Elevator Pitch] *"We're the only global organization that supports entrepreneurs of scale in different countries around the world."*

[Sector] **Industry agnostic**

[Description] Endeavor Miami helps South Florida entrepreneurs think bigger and make better decisions through access to mentors, capital, talent and a global market. "We're here to support underserved entrepreneurs and help them have an impact in their own communities," says Laura Maydon, managing director of Endeavor, the global nonprofit organization that has advised and helped scale more than eight hundred high-impact companies in thirty-two markets around the world. The Miami branch, launched in 2013 with help from Knight Foundation, was the first Endeavor organization in the United States.

Endeavor selects companies to be part of its ecosystem through an international panel on a rolling basis. Companies should be at the point of scale. The application process takes twelve to eighteen months, and candidates must pass a series of local and regional interviews before presenting to panelists from Endeavor's global business network. Companies accepted into the program receive tailored services from a volunteer network of global and local business leaders who serve as mentors, advisors, connectors, investors and role models. Endeavor, which doesn't take equity, seeks to supply all its businesses with mentorship, networks, strategic advice, talent, skills and inspiration. Over five years, Endeavor Miami has worked with twenty-three different businesses and forty-two cofounders. Laura hopes that within the next five years, Endeavor Miami businesses will be generating half a billion in revenue and five thousand jobs. "We measure our success through growth of the business but also what it provides to the greater community," Laura says.

Endeavor members are expected to pay it forward by helping to mentor the next generation of entrepreneurs after them. All members of the volunteer network are former founders selected by Endeavor, and Endeavor tracks the number of hours their volunteers dedicate throughout the course of the year. "We make sure to select the best entrepreneurs because we want them to be part of our network for a long time to come," Laura says.

[Apply to] endeavormiami.org/apply

[Links] Website: endeavormiami.org Facebook: endeavormiami Twitter: @EndeavorMIA

- **Fit the company.**
  This depends on the company we're building.
  For some companies, we're looking for someone
  to fill a more technical role, and for others, such
  as a sales platform, we're looking for someone
  with business-development experience.

- **Be active.**
  We're looking for the kind of people who want
  to make things happen and not sit around
  and wait for other people to tell them what to do.

- **Be gritty.**
  You must have that fire in your belly. That's
  something that's really hard to measure and really
  hard to evaluate, but we've been doing this for
  a long time.

- **Solve a big problem.**
  We're actively looking for opportunities in the four
  sectors where we're doing our events – logistics, real
  estate, travel and fintech – but that's not exclusive.
  What we want is a big idea that solves a real-world
  problem. Everything else is secondary.

LAB Miami Ventures

[Name]

[Elevator Pitch]

"We're building startups from scratch. We engage with companies to try to identify unsolved problems, and when we get an idea, we invest in it and work up to a prototype."

[Sector]

Travel and tourism, real estate, logistics and trade, fintech

[Description]

As the Miami tech ecosystem grows, LAB Ventures is sparking innovation out of South Florida. Still in its fledgling stage, LAB Ventures runs a company-building program out of The LAB, a coworking space in Wynwood that focuses on bringing together entrepreneurs and corporations to address their various pain points. "The idea is to create startups from scratch with our own capital and our own ideas, and then bring in a team and a cofounder once we have a working prototype," says Tigre Wenrich, CEO and executive director of LAB Ventures. "We then help that cofounder to grow the business up to a point where it can eventually raise outside capital from third parties."

Formally launched in 2017, LAB Ventures has built three companies so far: two are still in beta form, and one has gone on to receive external investment. The program provides entrepreneurs with a salary, a share in the company and the title of cofounder and CEO. It also offers an immense business development network, administrative support, mentoring and office space. "You don't own a majority of the company, but you make all the operating decisions and have a meaningful participation in the upside if it works," Tigre says.

LAB Ventures is sector agnostic, but actively seeks entrepreneurs in the verticals of tourism, real estate, logistics and trade and fintech, all of which align with the Miami market. The program fills a key gap for entrepreneurs and large corporations alike. "More and more, corporates want to engage with startups as a way to supplement their own internal innovation efforts," Tigre says. "They don't always know how to do it or how to find the most relevant startups for what they're looking for. And startups are always looking to establish relationships with large companies as a way to get business, and as a way to validate their technology. To the extent that we can provide that bridge, it's good for everyone."

[Apply to]

labventures.co

[Links]

Web: labventures.co Facebook: LABMiami Twitter: @thelabmiami Instagram: thelabmiami

- **Be sure you're solving a real problem.**
We're trying to serve real customers, such
as hospitals and payers. Bring us something
that moves the needle and solves a real problem
in the marketplace.

- **Demonstrate that you know your market.**
It's important that you know the details and dynamics
of your market and your chosen customer segment.

- **Show initial traction.**
We look for products that are ready to go, with at least
some sort of a pilot, and from there we help companies
scale that up.

- **Have a solid team.**
Having the right people in place is also important to us.

- **Have a polished pitch.**
We look for a sense of having things together.
Your pitch deck should be polished and presentable
and show a knowledge of the marketplace.

-
Talk to us before you apply.
The entrepreneurs who really stand out are the ones
who take the time to connect with us before it's time
for selection.

[Name]
Startupbootcamp

[Elevator Pitch] *"We're a global entrepreneur-support organization that runs a variety of programs, including accelerators, scale programs and corporate-engagement programs. SBC Scale Digital Health Miami is one of our scale programs. We help growth-stage companies grow and gain traction in the healthcare marketplace."*

[Sector] Healthcare

[Description] Startupbootcamp programs can be found all around the world, in more than a dozen countries from the US to China, with programs that specifically cater to the populations being served. In Mumbai, that means the financial services sector. In Hartford, it's insurance. So what attracted the organization to Miami? The potential to disrupt the huge and still growing healthcare market. "We decided to focus on healthcare because Miami is this incredibly diverse place that's also this big consumer of everything healthcare," says Allan Daisley, managing director of Startupbootcamp Digital Health Miami. "There's racial diversity, linguistic diversity, a large socio-economic gap and a pronounced old and young divide."

Startupbootcamp Digital Health Miami was the first program offering in the US (the company now also runs programs in New York, Hartford and San Francisco). It helps guide growth-stage healthcare companies through a six-month, mostly remote program that gives them access to coworking space, seed funding, mentorship opportunities and implementation partnerships with healthcare companies, as well as connecting them to a network of corporate partners, investors and entrepreneurs from around the world. Startups typically spend one week on-site and three weeks remotely where they're given time and resources to scale their business.

Many startups that go through the program address a social need present in the Miami community and beyond. Examples include Wellth, an app that uses behavioral economics and habit-formation research to incentivize patients to take their medicines; and Mediconecta, a Latin America-focused telehealth provider platform. With twenty hospitals and one thousand life sciences companies, as well as a high eligibility of both Medicare and Medicaid patients, Miami is the perfect testing grounds for this up-and-coming technology. "For the startups, it's an opportunity to make measurable progress and raise revenues," Allan says. "There are a lot of opportunities to make a difference here in Miami. We have many people who are not getting the healthcare they need."

[Apply to] startupbootcamp.org

[Links] Web: startupbootcamp.org Facebook: ScaleDigitalHealthMiami Twitter: @sbcHealth

- **Have market validation.**
  The ROI for VCs is often similar to the ROI for corporate partnerships. It's hard to pitch a startup that doesn't have market validation and traction.

- **Be in a growth market.**
  Being in a large market that has a multibillion dollar market cap is a really interesting opportunity for a corporate.

- **Differentiate your product.**
  What does the startup offer that's unique enough to make it attractive for a corporate to say, "I can't do this on my own; I really need to look into forming a strategic partnership or B2B relationship with the startup?'"

- **Be defensible.**
  You should have your IP protected and have your p's and q's together in terms of core business readiness.

- **Have a strong team.**
  Does the strength of your team demonstrate to a corporate that they're not going to take a significant risk on an important partnership opportunity?

[Name]
Venture Café Miami

[Elevator Pitch]
"We're a nonprofit organization that seeks to grow Miami's innovation community by working to make it more diverse, inclusive, accessible and better connected locally, nationally and globally."

[Sector]
Multiple

[Description]
Offering multiple programs for startups and other players in the startup ecosystem, Venture Café Miami serves up innovation and inclusion, all on the same plate. Its main program, the #ThursdayGathering, brings together tech and innovation leaders, budding entrepreneurs, investors, educators and more in an intentional and inclusive setting that's open and free to all. Since 2016, the organization has impacted almost 30,000 innovators and collaborated with over 700 organizations to curate over 1,500 innovation-related sessions.

But Venture Café Miami is more than just a once-per-week affair. For the past year, the organization has worked to bring together large corporations and smaller startups through its Captains of Innovation program, in partnership with Venture Café Global Institute and the Cambridge Innovation Center. The idea behind the program, according to Leigh-Ann Buchanan, founding executive director of Venture Café Miami, is to "leverage our relationships, particularly around the #ThursdayGathering, to create meaningful connections, B2B matching, and opportunities for global companies that need to better understand what trends and opportunities are around a particular industry vertical or issue."

During the program, large companies work with startups in high-growth industries (such as trade and logistics, life sciences and health care, hospitality and tourism, and aviation and aerospace) to complete an "innovation sprint," collaborate on ideation and engage with one another through community visits, conferences and trend-mapping sessions. The best way for startups to get involved, Leigh-Ann says, is for them to familiarize themselves with the broader Venture Café Miami ecosystem by attending #ThursdayGatherings, presenting at demo days and pitch competitions, and plugging into local investor networks. "What Captains is trying to do at its core is shift the narrative and the modalities of engagement for corporates and create the infrastructure for them to be meaningful partners," Leigh-Ann says. "It's about encouraging corporates to avoid 'innovation tourism' from an elevated position and instead saying, 'We're here to make you a part of this entrepreneurial community.'"

[Apply to]
venturecafemiami.org, info@venturecafemiami.org

[Links]
Web: venturecafemiami.org Facebook: VentureCafeMiami Twitter: @VentureCafeMIA

- **Create new layers to the culinary ecosystem in Miami.**
  Do something new. Make something that's cutting edge, and then focus on doing that one thing really well.

- **Be ready to handle the heat.**
  We're looking for operational efficiency, for startups that can handle large amounts of people, environmental pressures and other dynamics.

- **Understand what community means.**
  You have to want to be part of a collaborative community. You are one hub that's part of the larger wheel.

- **Come ready to learn.**
  How do you think your business could benefit or what would you like to learn from the chef mentors and/or business mentors who offer their free expertise to The Wynwood Yard businesses?

The Wynwood Yard

[Name]

[Elevator Pitch] *"Built for our community, as a reflection of our community, we're an incubator that supports local entrepreneurs, celebrates Miami's vibrant culture and fosters tolerance and diversity. We serve as a platform for community-building around arts, culture, entrepreneurship and sustainability."*

[Sector] Hospitality, food, drink, social venture

[Description] Located on 40,000 ft2 in the heart of the Wynwood Arts District, The Wynwood Yard is an ecosystem all on its own. Brightly colored food trucks serve up everything from Hawaiian poké bowls to Brazilian rodizio sausages. Vendors sell artisanal local handmade jewelry. Customers gather at picnic tables surrounded by lush vegetation and bathed in the faint orange glow of hanging lights. During the day, school students are invited to learn about urban farming. At night, the space hosts events – over one thousand each year – ranging from musical performances to social impact gatherings. Almost every one of the Yard's events is created in collaboration with a local arts, cultural, environmental or fitness entrepreneurs, drawing people from every walk of life. What customers may not realize is that Wynwood Yard also serves as a culinary incubator for food startups. "I'm passionate about about lowering barriers to entry for local startups in the food, beverage and creative sectors," says founder Della Heiman.

Founded in the summer of 2015 as an incubation hub, event space and community garden all in one, the space was initially home to a handful of businesses. The idea was for Della and her team to manage the day-to-day operations and deal with overhead and to "let entrepreneurs do what they do best." That technique has led to a blossoming of success, with more than two hundred talented food entrepreneurs cycling through the space. By being a part of the program, food startups receive external promotion and marketing training, mentorship in cooking and business, and access to amenities, events and resources, and they're plunged headlong into operating a full-service pop-up, catering to a constant mill of customers. "We have a huge array of culinary talent from around the world," Della says. "The space fosters diversity and promotes tolerance. You see people from all different walks of life mixing, interacting, and getting to know one other. It's a beautiful melting pot and great symbol of what Miami is." In late Spring 2019, The Wynwood Yard will close its gates to transition to a dynamic new neighborhood in Miami. Its will continue to evolve with new projects rooted in the community-centered magic of entrepreneurial incubation, live music, community events, and sustainability-focused programming.

[Apply to] thewynwoodyard.com/apply

[Links] Web: thewynwoodyard.com Facebook: thewynwoodyard Instagram: wynwoodyard

ces

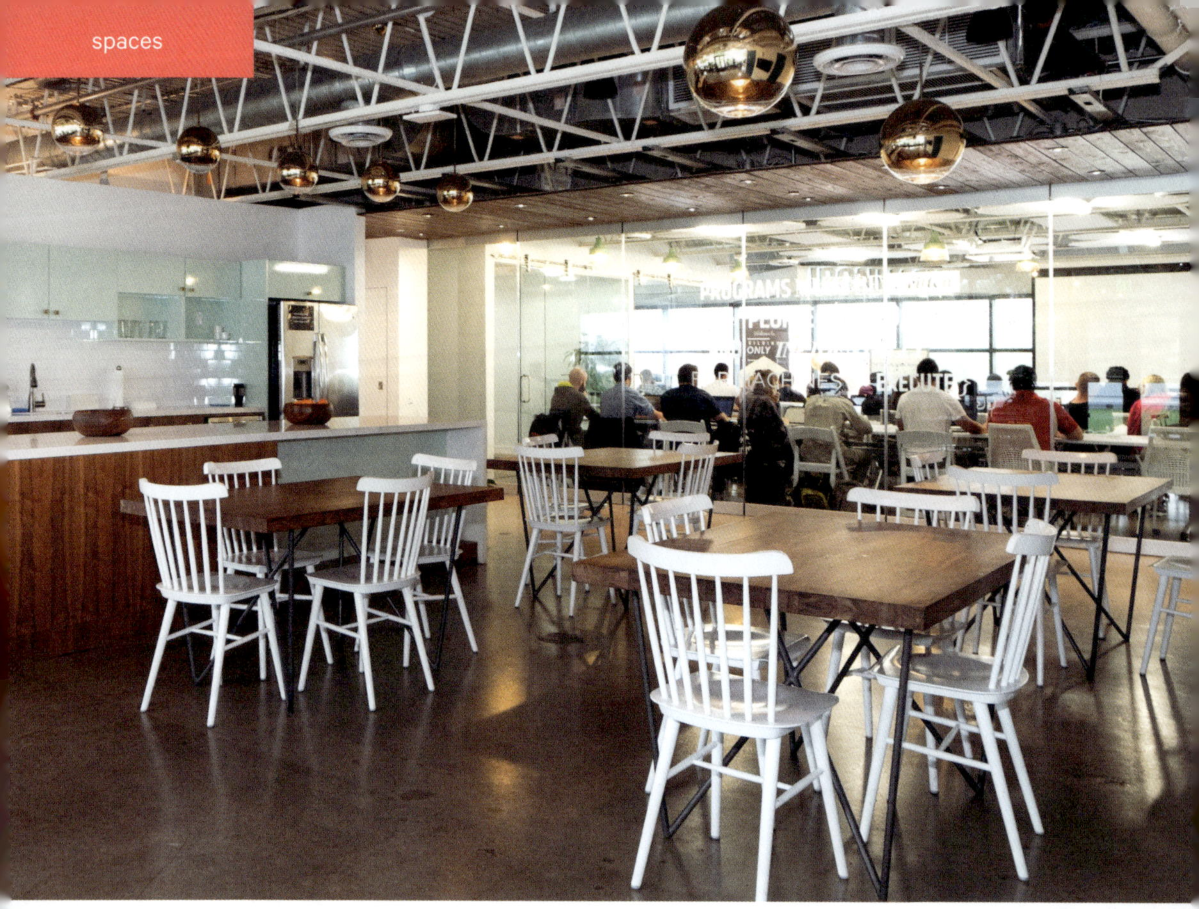

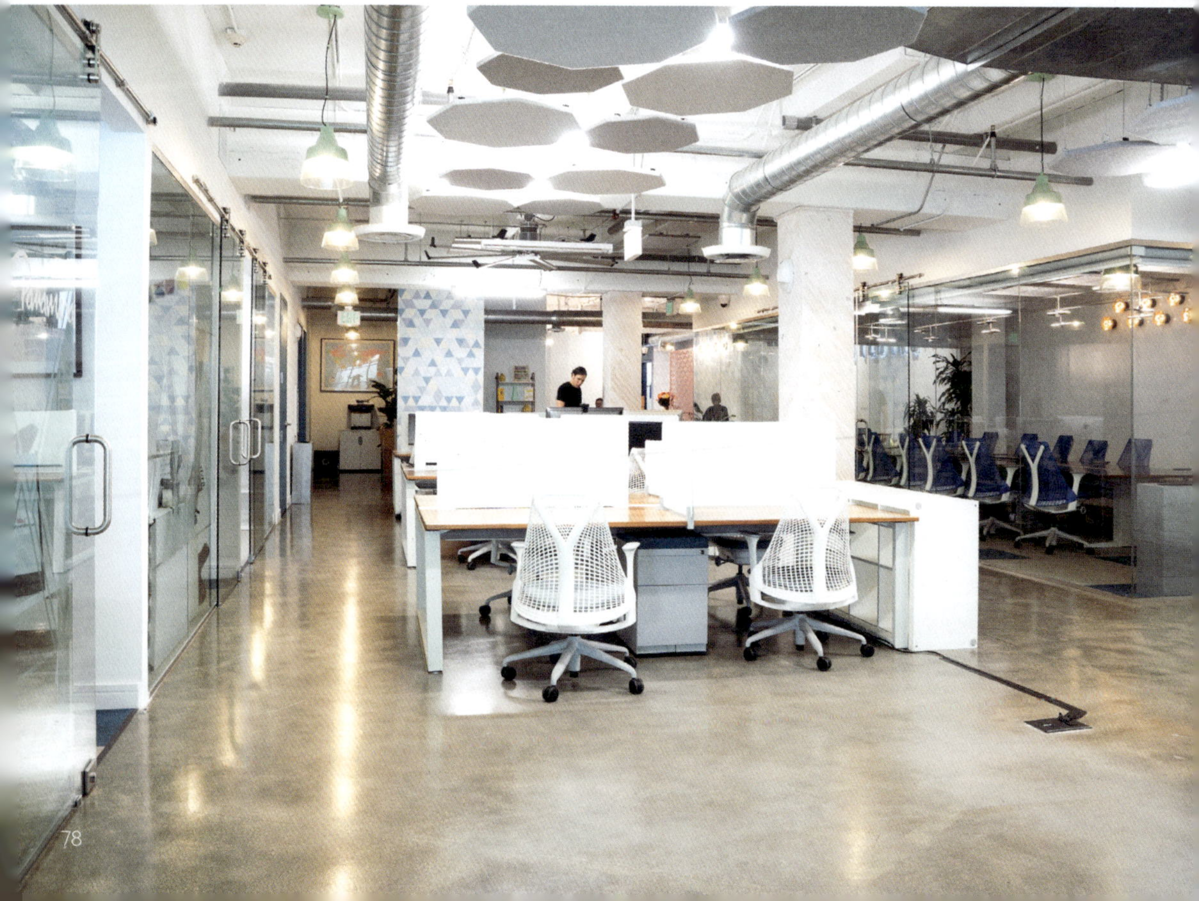

[Name] # BUILDING

[Address] 120 SW 8th St., Miami, FL, 33130

[Total Area]

1,300M²

[Workspaces]

74

[The Story] Upon entering BUILDING, Miami's palm trees quickly give way to a more Silicon Valley vibe. A coworking space designed for later-stage tech companies, BUILDING features industrial ceilings, an unobtrusive blue-and-white color scheme and a sleek, minimalist design. Located in Brickell, Miami's business district, BUILDING was founded as a space for serious tech entrepreneurs to come together, ideate and work hard on their own products in the company of other like-minded innovators. "The fact that everyone is working in tech and there's only one location lends itself to strong connections," says Rebecca Willett, general manager at BUILDING. "All of our members are pretty serious about what it is they're doing." While the vibe is business forward, members have fun, too – Miami style. The third floor features a spacious roof-deck replete with turf, picnic tables, and cornhole games.

The coworking space, which opened in 2015, was founded by the same entrepreneurs who launched and sold the .CO domain extension: Jose "Hutch" Rasco and Juan Diego Calle. Their idea was to give back to the burgeoning Miami tech scene by providing a physical space for entrepreneurs. Along with coworking space, BUILDING also hosts events, panels and meetups. "What makes BUILDING really unique is the community aspect of having different members of the tech ecosystem in one space, and how they end up organically becoming friends, clients and supporters of each other," Rebecca says.

[Links] Web: building.co Facebook: BUILDINGMiami Twitter: @buildingco Instagram: buildingco

THERE IS NO ELEVATOR TO SUCCESS, YOU HAVE TO TAKE THE STAIRS

Face of the Space:

Rebecca Willett is the general manager of BUILDING. She's currently writing her MBA thesis for the University of Palermo in Argentina, and she comes to BUILDING with a mix of experience, including as a freelance writer and a business dev-elopment fellow at a Colombian startup.

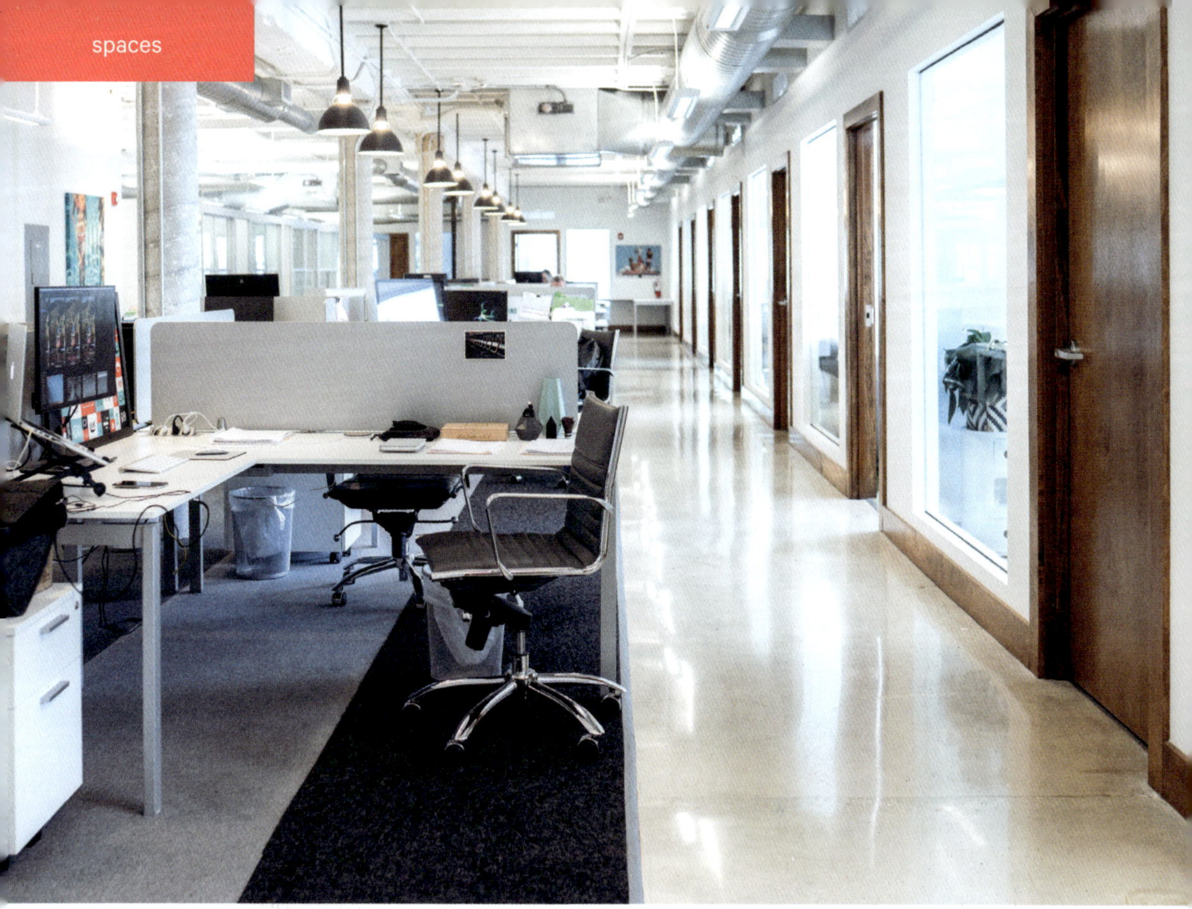

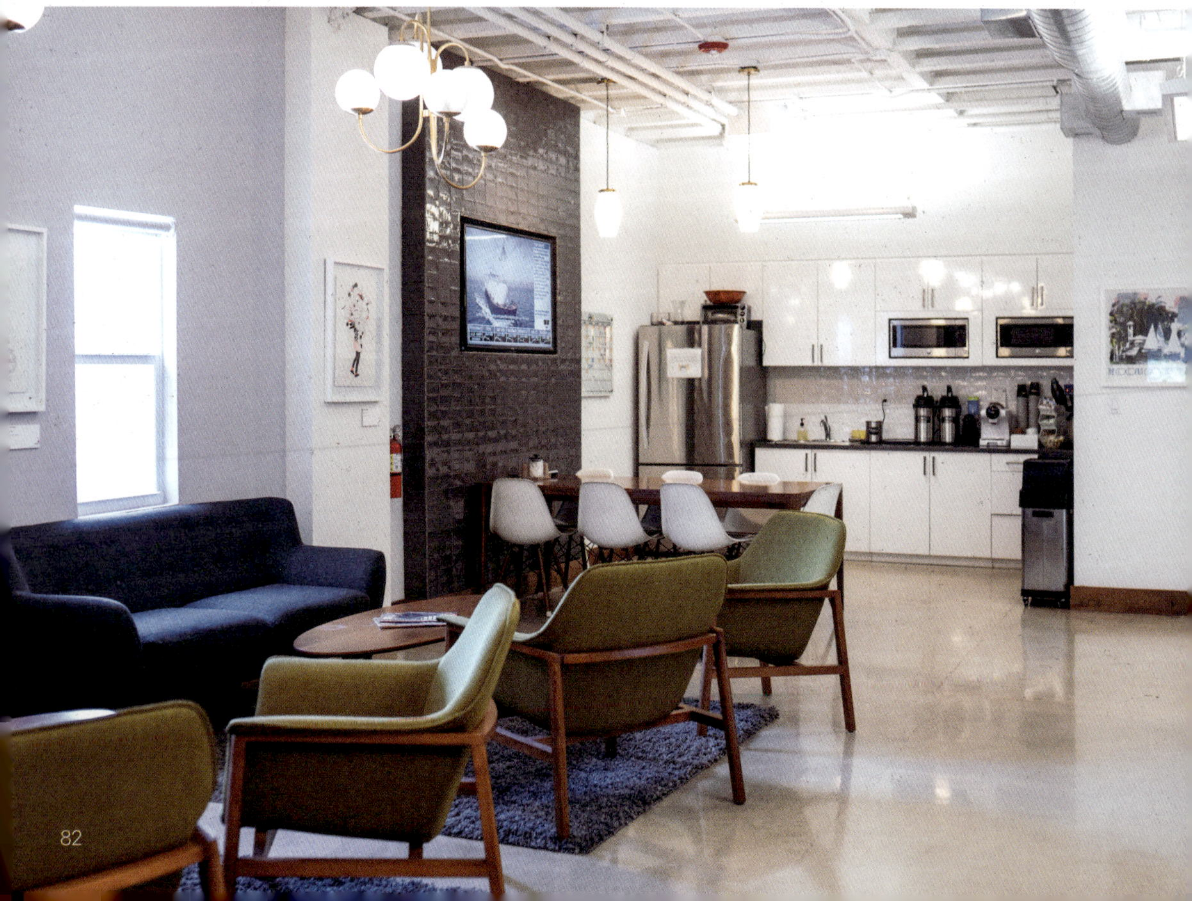

[Name] Büro Coconut Grove

[Address] 2980 McFarlane Road, Coconut Grove, Florida 33133

[Total Area]

1,021 M²

[Workspaces]

150

[The Story] Büro (German for "office") is a purveyor of boutique coworking spaces aimed at nurturing the startup ecosystem in Miami. Founder Michael Feinstein opened the first location in 2010 after realizing the lack of available space for Miami's entrepreneurial and freelance community. The business has grown to encompass six different locations across South Florida, with each space taking on the unique flavor and vibe of its neighborhood. "We want to be a catalyst for up-and-coming neighborhoods," says Büro's Director of Operations Masha Grinberg. "People should be able to walk around, eat, drink and play in the same neighborhood where they work, and we provide them with that."

Büro Coconut Grove is designed to honor the history of the neighborhood it resides in. The space contains thirty-three offices of varying sizes and twenty individual workstations along with open work areas, lounges, conference rooms, phone booths and a reception area. The office has a "modern and artsy vibe," Grinberg says, and is within walking distance of dozens of restaurants, cafes and boutiques. All Büro members at all locations have access to monthly workshops and events, and receive discounts and perks at popular local businesses. Büro focuses on boutique-style spaces, with no location larger than twenty thousand square feet. In total, Büro boasts over one thousand members across a variety of different industries.

[Links] Web: buromiami.com Facebook: buromiami Twitter: @buromiami Instagram: buromiami

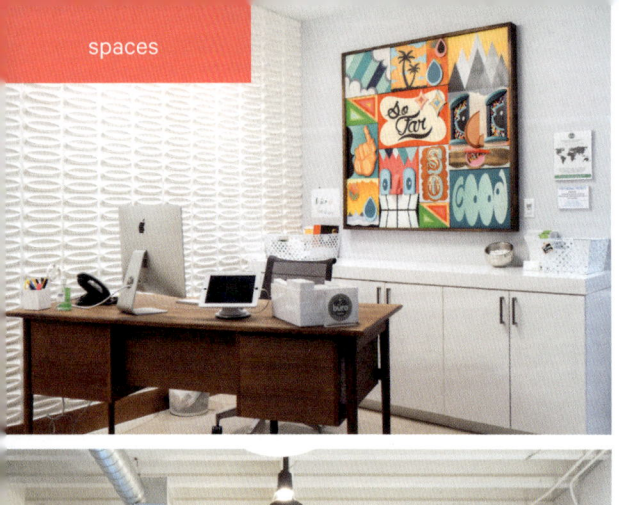

Face of the Space:

Michael Feinstein is from Montreal, Canada. Prior to founding Büro, he worked in hospitality overseeing hotel projects and villa developments around the world. Previous to that he worked in corporate development for American Express. Michael holds a bachelor's degree from Cornell University and an MBA from INSEAD.

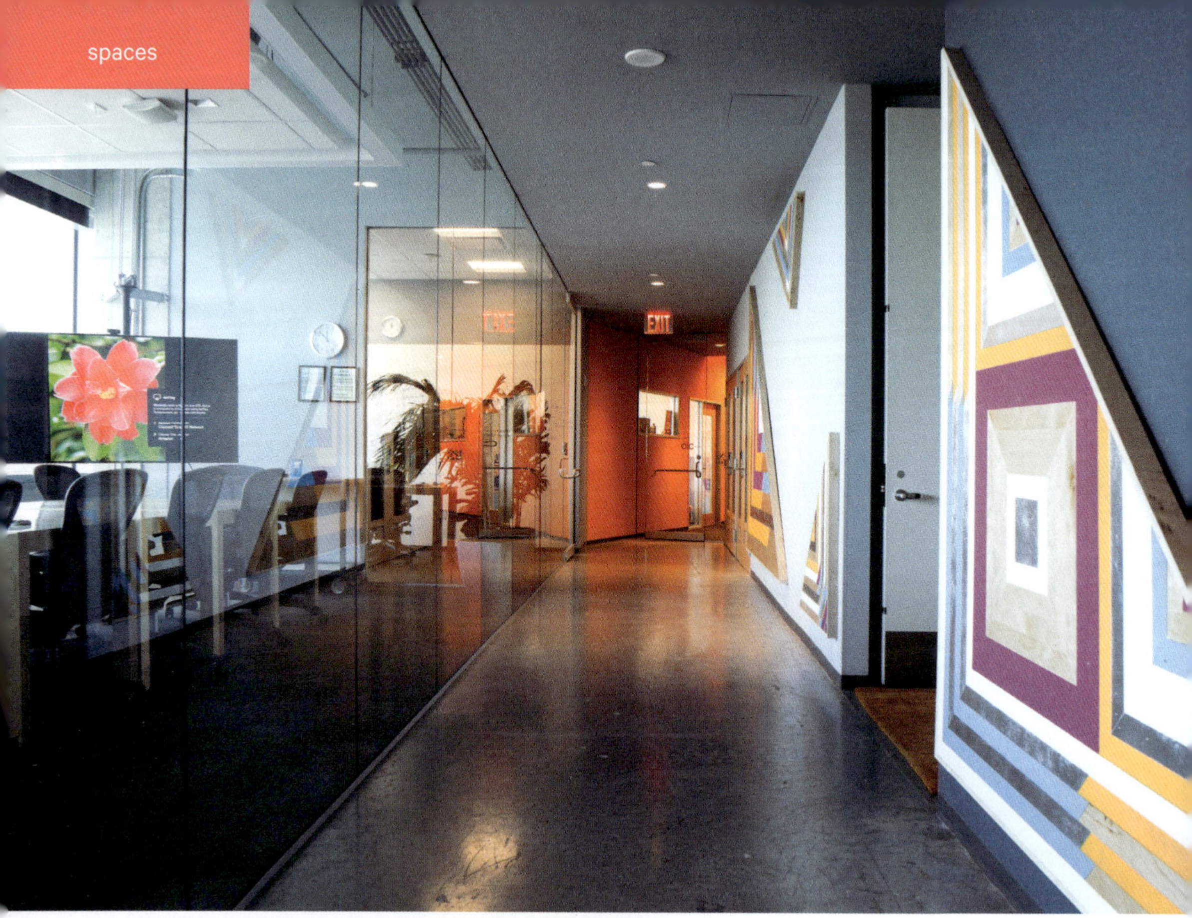
EXIT

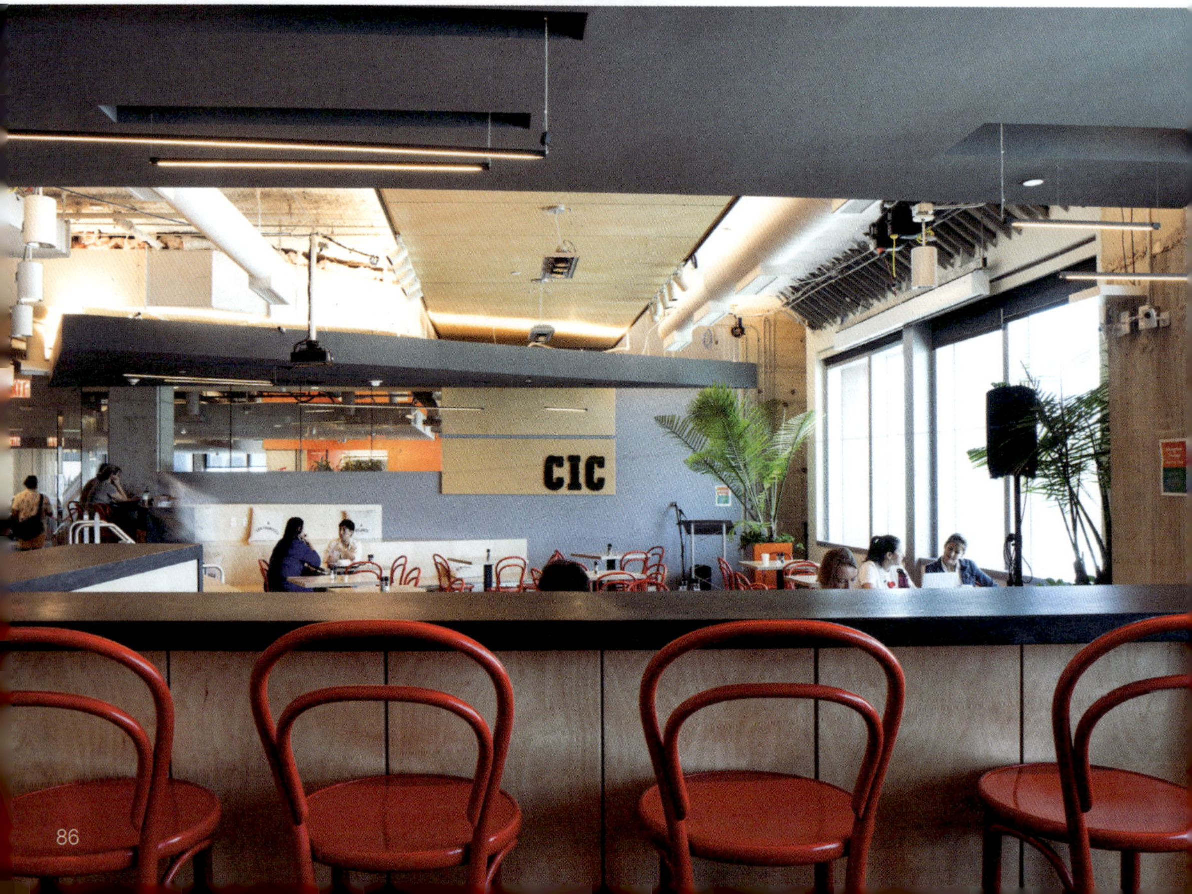
CIC

[Name] # CIC Miami

[Address] 1951 NW 7th Avenue, Suite 600, Miami, FL 33136

[Total Area]

7,400M²

[Workspaces]

800

[The Story] Located in what was formerly the University of Miami's Life Science & Technology Park building, CIC Miami puts a new twist on an old science. From its shimmering exterior to its light- and plant-filled interior, the space serves as a hub for innovators across multiple fields, from life sciences to fintech, academia and investing. Replete with shared laboratories, a shared kitchen, common spaces and the only wet lab south of Orlando, CIC Miami is home to approximately 280 companies. These include The *New Tropic*, a magazine covering South Florida tech; Cargo 42, which runs an on-demand trucking service; and Radical Partners, a social impact accelerator. The colorful space has a mostly open layout with nooks for hanging out and offices for larger companies. "We spend a lot of energy on how we design our spaces," says Natalia Martinez-Kalinina, general manager at CIC Miami.

Founded in 2016, CIC Miami forms part of Cambridge Innovation Center's global network, which includes Boston, St. Louis, Philadelphia, Providence, Rotterdam and Warsaw. The space is home to events such as the weekly #ThursdayGathering, hosted by Venture Café, as well hackathons, networking meetups and workshops. "What we do extends way beyond the physical infrastructure," Natalia says. "We love having physical clients, but the core of what we do is figuring out how to leverage the space for other things that add value to the ecosystem."

[Links] Web: cic.com/miami Facebook: cicmiami Twitter: @CIC_Miami Instagram: cicmiami

Face of the Space:

Natalia Martinez-Kalinina is the general manager at CIC Miami and the founder of Awesome Foundation and Aminta Ventures. With a degree in social-organizational psychology from Columbia University, Natalia's interests lie in group dynamics: What drives groups of people to behave in one way or another? Before starting at CIC Miami, she spent several years looking at the Miami tech ecosystem from this lens. When CIC expanded to Miami, she was able to marry together all of the things she really cares about.

ORE MAKERS
MOONLIGHTER
moonlighter.co
eat
drink
collaborate

FROST SCIENCE
EXIT

[Name]
Moonlighter

[Address] 2041 NW 1st Place, Miami FL, 33127

[Total Area]

325 M²

[Workspaces]

46

[The Story] Moonlighter is a community-based fabrication lab, creative coworking space and STEAM (science, technology, engineering, arts and mathematics) learning center that aspires to empower Miami makers with the tools, technologies and skill-building opportunities to create almost anything. The business was started by Miami couple Tom Pupo and Daisy Nodal. The duo had become familiar with the concept of makerspaces while studying abroad in Europe. They decided to bring the concept to Miami in 2015 so their community would have access to design software and advanced manufacturing tools. "We knew Miami had a maker community, and we built this for them," Tom says. "We're the only coworking space in town where you can come in, make a mess and really build something physical."

Moonlighter is equipped with 3D printers, CNC mills, a laser cutter, power tools, a lathe, drill presses, sewing machines, vinyl cutters, a circuitry and electronics lab and an eco-materials lab. The makerspace is accessible to anyone in the community who wants to learn how to use the tools, and entrepreneurs in the midst of prototyping can also rent office space. Tom and Daisy place a strong emphasis on education, offering workshops for both kids and adults. "We want this to be a comfortable and approachable space for people new to design," Tom says. "We want to be a resource for all of Miami."

[Links] **Web:** moonlighter.co **Facebook:** moonlightermiami **Twitter:** @MoonlighterMIA

Face of the Space:

Daisy Nodal (CEO) and Tom Pupo (COO) are
the cofounders of Moonlighter. They're both
Miami natives who have lived in the area
their entire lives. They graduated together
from Florida International University with
masters degrees in architecture and have now
dedicated their careers to building up Miami
with their social enterprise.

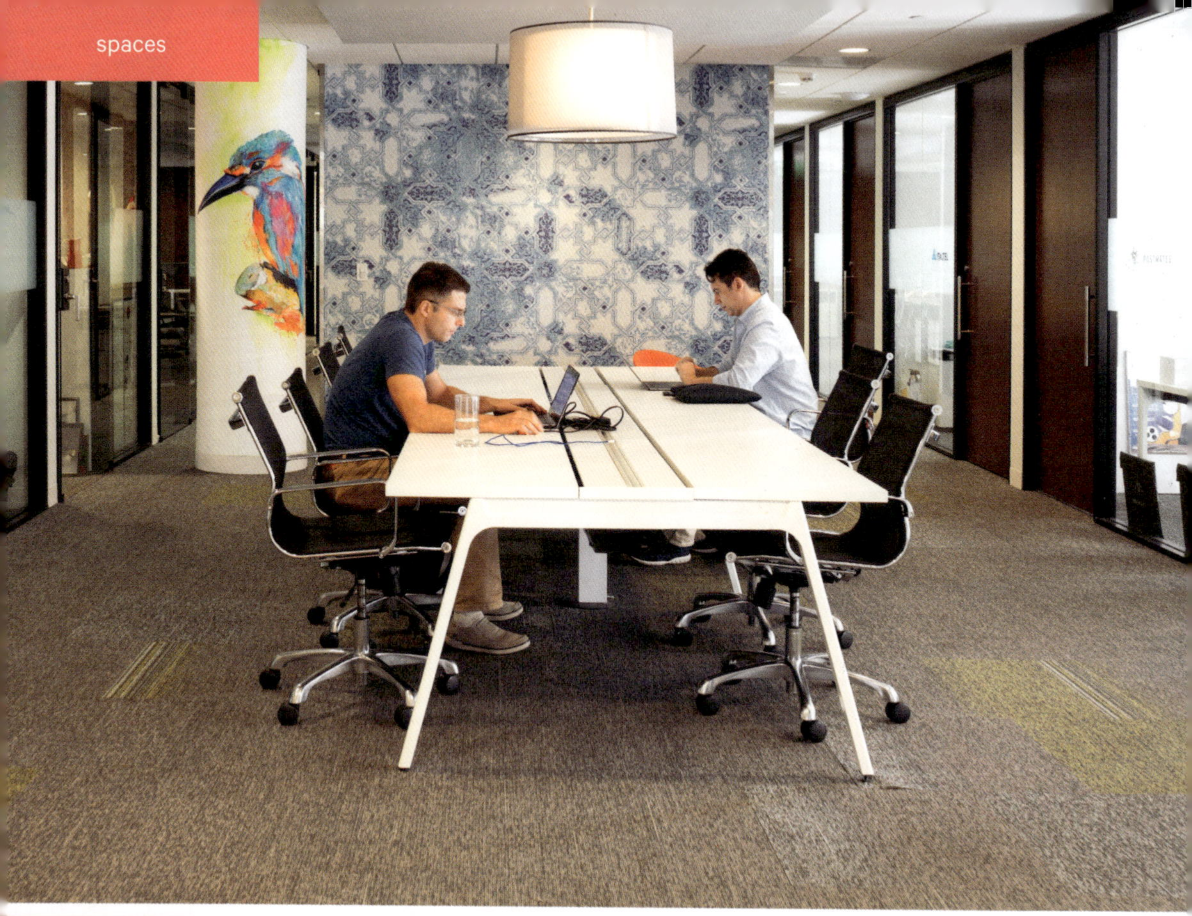

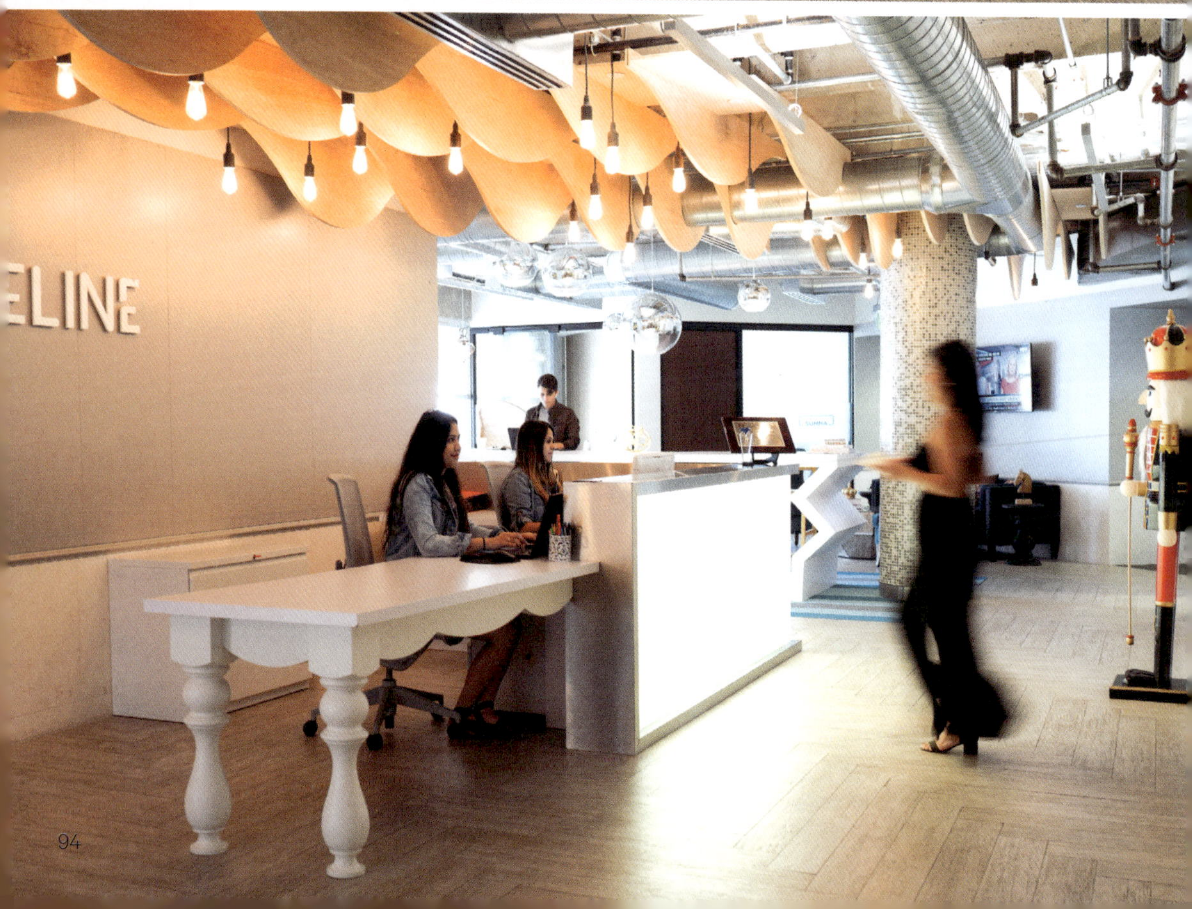
ELINE

[Name] # Pipeline Workspaces

[Address]   95 Merrick Way, 3rd Floor, Coral Gables, FL 33134

[Total Area]

1,250M²

[Workspaces]

200

[The Story]   At Pipeline Coral Gables, the beauty is in the details: an ornate candelabra on the reception desk, a Castilian coat of arms, a life-sized statue of a mustachioed king in the entryway. The space hearkens back to the past, while at the same time looking squarely toward the future. Undular wooden slats hang from the ceiling, creating an oceanic ambiance. Floor-to-ceiling windows let in natural light and provide a view of the palm trees outside. Elegant conference rooms are equipped with modern features that make doing business easier. "We've developed a high-end space where real businesses interact and grow," says Philippe Houdard, cofounder of Pipeline Workspaces. "Our concept has always been focused on creating value by fostering the interchange among companies."

Founded in 2012, Pipeline Workspaces now has seven locations across the US: six in Florida (downtown Miami, Coral Gables, Fort Lauderdale, Doral, Orlando and Tampa) and one in Philadelphia. Its members include companies large and small, including Google, Uber, Spotify, Postmates and HBO. As the company has grown, it has stayed true to its mission of bringing people together. "There's a sea change in the way that people work," Philippe says. "People are yearning to connect with others to make life richer and make the likelihood of success greater, and that's what we strive to do."

[Links]   **Web:** pipelineworkspaces.com **Facebook:** PipelineWorkspaces **Twitter:** @PipelineSpaces

Face of the Space:

Philippe Houdard is an entrepreneur, philanthropist and investor. In 2012, he and his business partner Todd Oresky founded Pipeline Workspaces. Before that, Philippe founded SkyBank Financial, which helps businesses with electronic financial transactions, and the Developing Minds Foundation, an education nonprofit. "I've experienced the trials and tribulations of the startup world," Philippe says. "I recognize the challenges of starting and growing a business with the restrictions of working out of an isolated space."

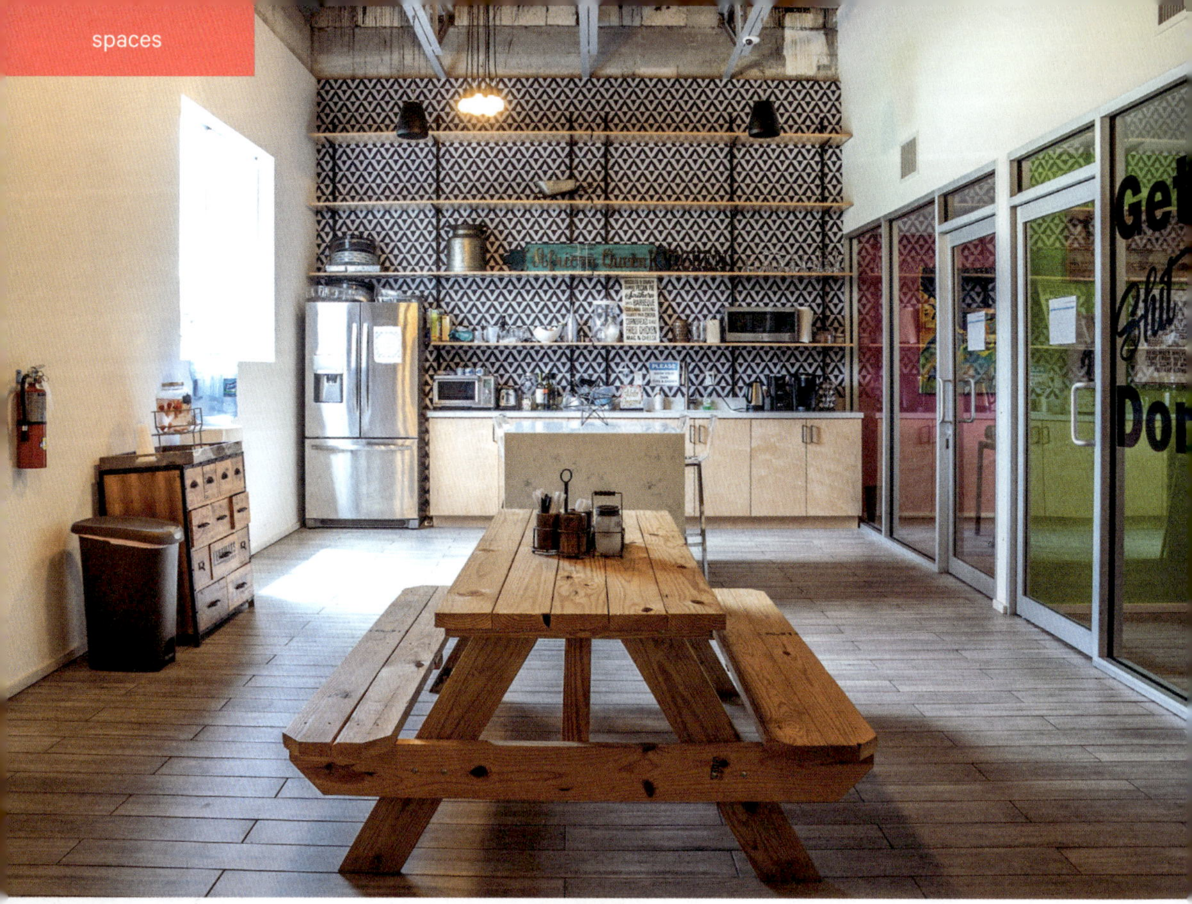

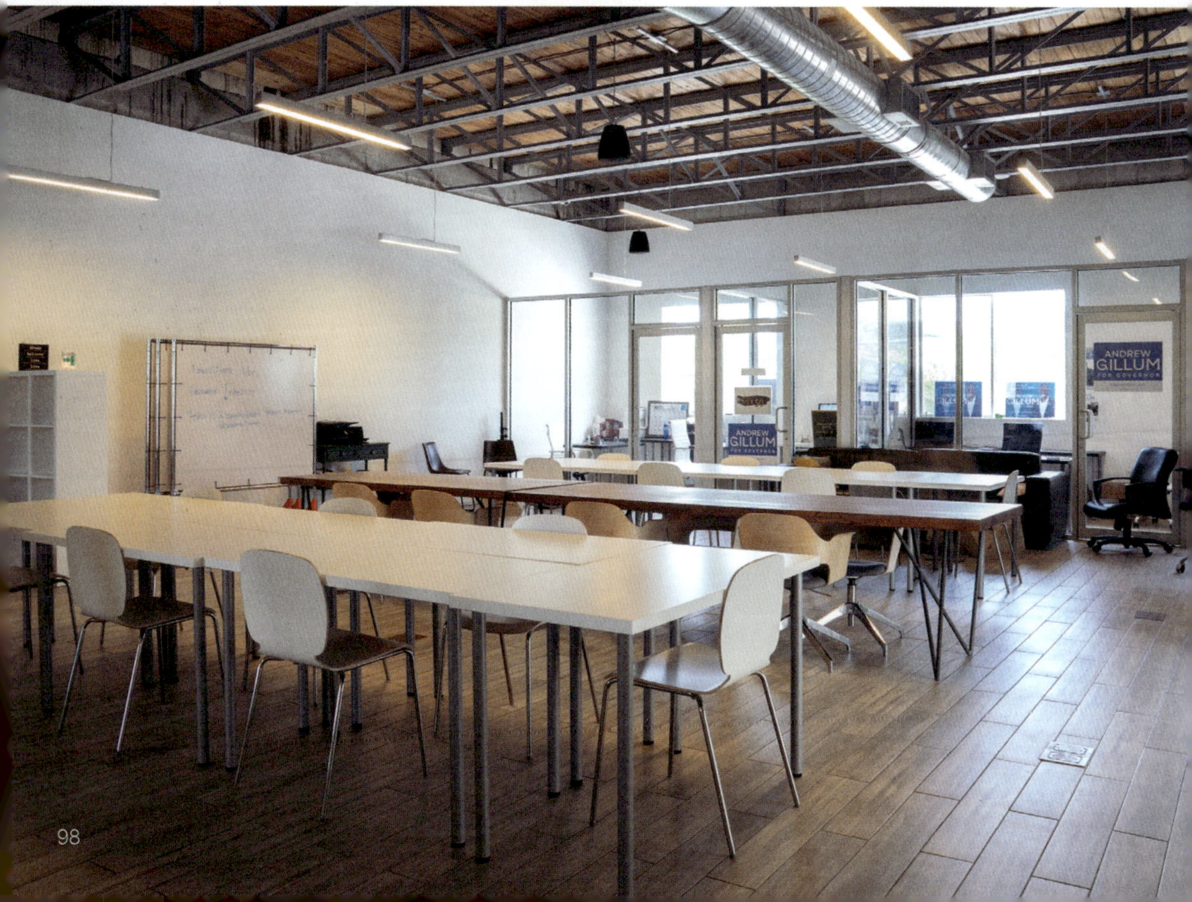
ANDREW
GILLUM

[Name] # Space Called Tribe

[Address]   937 NW 3rd Ave, Miami, FL 33136

[Total Area]

930M²

[Workspaces]

50

[The Story]   Located in Overtown, Space Called Tribe is reclaiming a piece of the past to pave a way for the community's future. One year ago, the space – a former Masonic lodge with historical designation – lay dormant. Now the two-floor building brims with life. Code Fever Miami, which operates the space, brought in muralist M. Blake to bring style to the white walls in the lobby. It worked with a community sponsor to install conference rooms, a coworking area, private offices, a kitchen, classrooms, a relaxation space and a rock garden. Since last December, twelve companies – spanning sectors from wellness to marketing – have moved into the shared coworking space.

Code Fever Miami works to bridge the economic gap within the minority community. It does this through intentional programming aimed at increasing diversity in the startup ecosystem, and it hosts events focused on community redevelopment, emerging technologies and more. "We are on a mission to rid our communities of innovation deserts and give a place for minorities to grow as entrepreneurs," says Ryan Hall, community manager for Space Called Tribe. "Over the past few years with Code Fever and Black Tech Week, we've worked to cultivate a community of hundreds of speakers and thousands of attendees, and now we finally have a dedicated space for all of these minority business owners to meet, work, collaborate and network."

[Links]   Web: spacecalledtribe.com Facebook: spacecalledtribe Instagram: spacecalledtribe

Face of the Space:

In addition to serving as Space Called Tribe's community manager, Ryan Hall is also the program manager at Code Fever Miami. He has been with Code Fever Miami since its infancy, working in media, instruction and community outreach. "You meet the craziest mixture of people: from freelance designers to venture capitalists to owners of different companies," Ryan says. "You never know who's going to walk in the door every day."

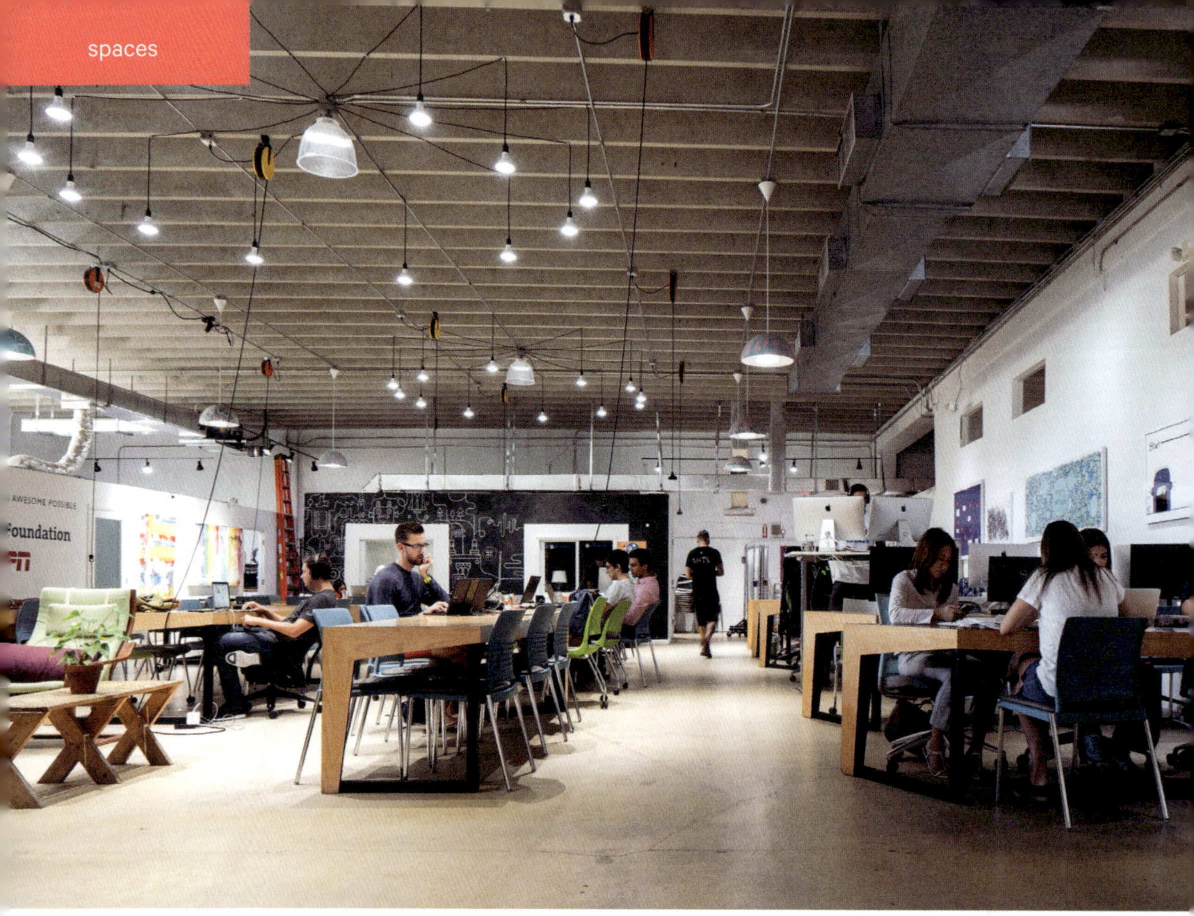
Foundation

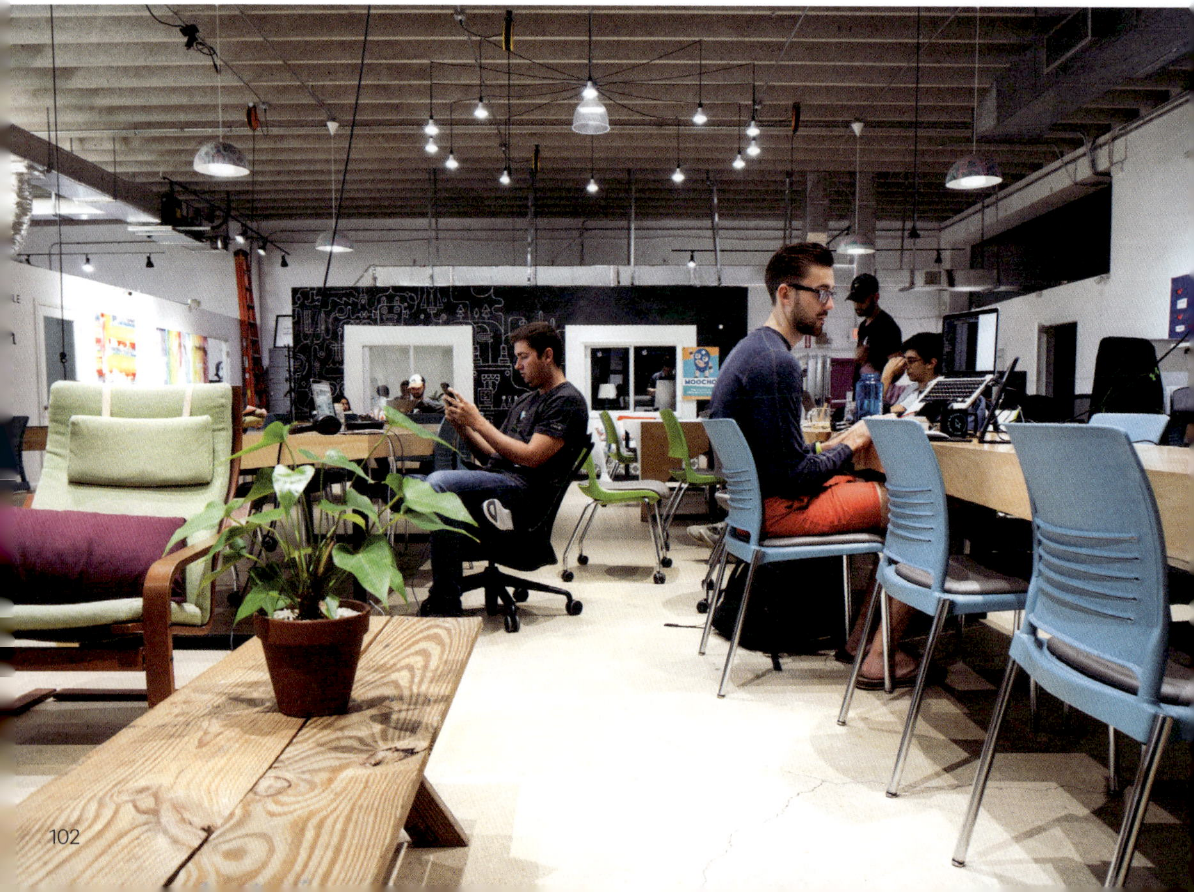

[Name]

The LAB Miami

[Address]   400 NW 26th St., Miami, Florida 33127

[Total Area]

930M²

[Workspaces]

200

[The Story]   Miami's once edgy Wynwood neighborhood has transformed into a trendy arts district on the rise for entrepreneurs – and The LAB is a big part of why. The LAB, located across the street from Zak the Baker cafe and next to the Miami Light Project community theater, is a 10,000 ft² (930 m²) space in the heart of Wynwood, offering coworking, community events, networking opportunities, parking and more to its 150 members, which include startups, corporations, artists and nonprofits. The space, an airy, bare-bones industrial warehouse adorned with local art and featuring handcrafted desks and gallery-style murals, was once used for manufacturing energy drinks. Maybe there's still something lingering in the air, because that vibe has stuck to this day. "You just feel the energy when you come here," says Rachael Bickford, managing director at The LAB.

Founded in 2012, The LAB was the first coworking space to open in Miami. It remains locally owned and operated, and it frequently opens its doors to the broader community for events, such as during Art Basel, an annual art festival. The LAB offers fifteen private offices, four call rooms, two conference rooms, two large open spaces (The Arena for coworking, and The Living Room for events) and a fully landscaped outdoor oasis called the Idea Garden. Membership options start at $150 per month.

[Links]   Web: thelabmiami.com Facebook: LABMiami Twitter: @thelabmiami Instagram: thelabmiami

Face of the Space:

Rachael Bickford, managing director at The LAB, graduated from the College of Charleston with a degree in business administration and moved to Miami with her real estate license to sell executive office space. Not long after, she was contacted by a member of The LAB, and immediately fell in love with the company. "I saw what it was and thought it was the coolest thing ever," Rachael says. "I accepted the offer and have been here ever since."

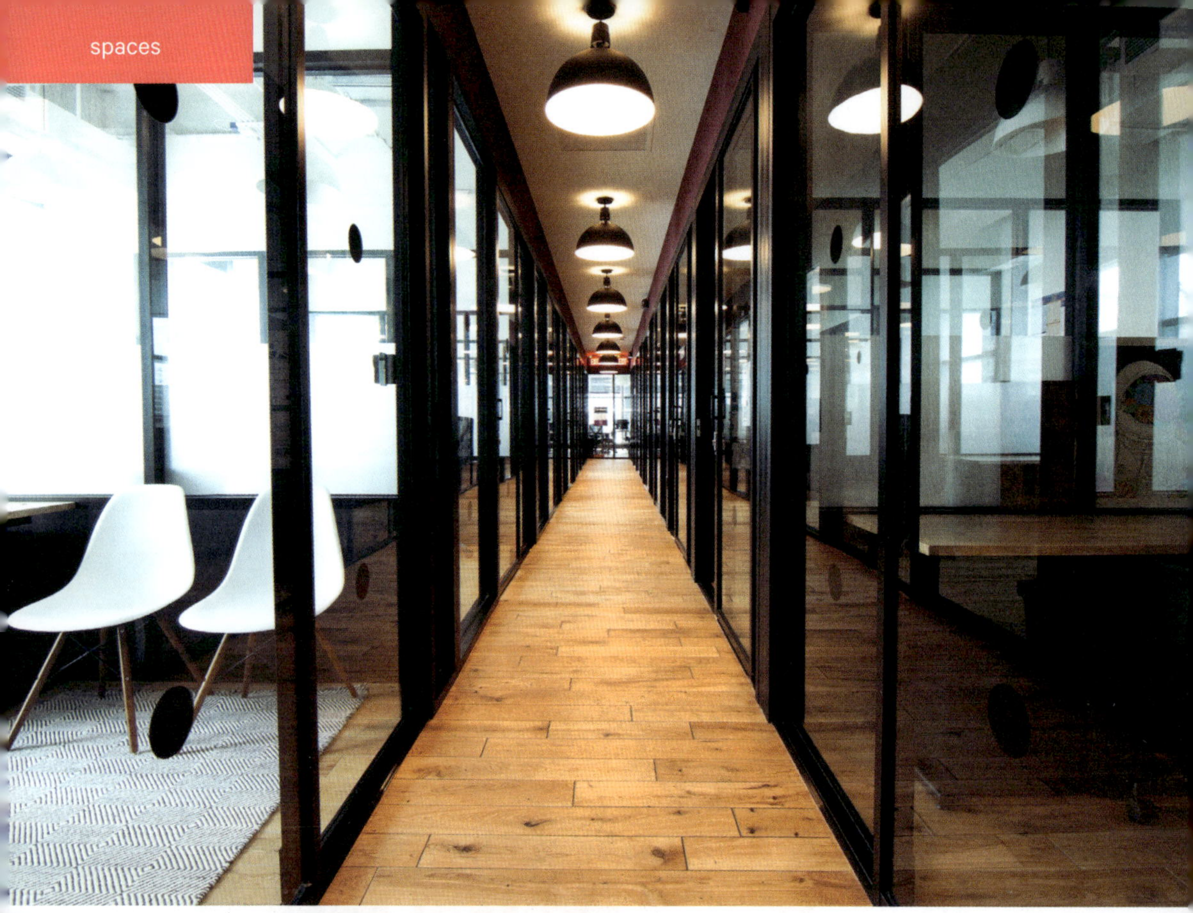

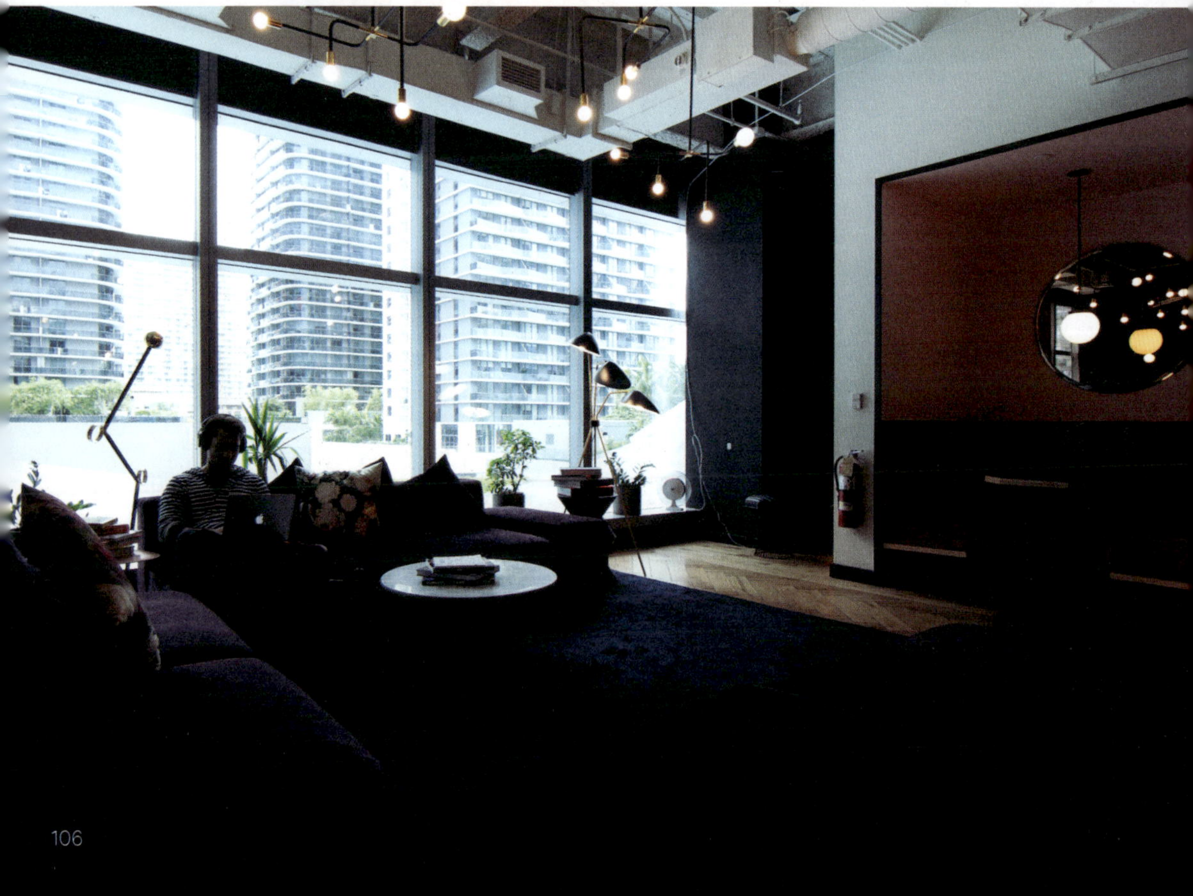

[Name] # WeWork Miami

[Address] 78 SW 7th Street, Miami FL, 33130

[Total Area]

7,000M²

[Workspaces]

1,400

[The Story] Global company, local playbook: that's WeWork's motto, and perhaps nowhere has this been better illustrated than in the Miami area, which has seen five WeWork locations spring up in the past several years, each with a different vibe and different décor but the same mission. From downtown to Coral Gables and everywhere in between, WeWork locations are like architectural and social chameleons, blending into the surroundings and providing a home for collaboration, innovation and networking. Lincoln Road features bright colors and a tropical feel, while at the South of Fifth WeWork marina elements abound. "When you first walk in, each building in Miami has its own personality," says Anna Prisse, Miami community manager at WeWork. "Then, the programming of the space – the way in which we activate the space for our members and our communities – involves listening to our members, understanding what it is that they're looking for, and tailoring our programming around that."

In the Brickell City Centre location, jewel-toned, ruby and emerald design elements play off the prefab construction of the Brickell City Centre retail complex itself. From this location, WeWork members can step out onto a lively terrace to take in the view of the innovative, sustainable architecture of the Swire Properties-owned mall complex, as well as look toward downtown Miami and the river.

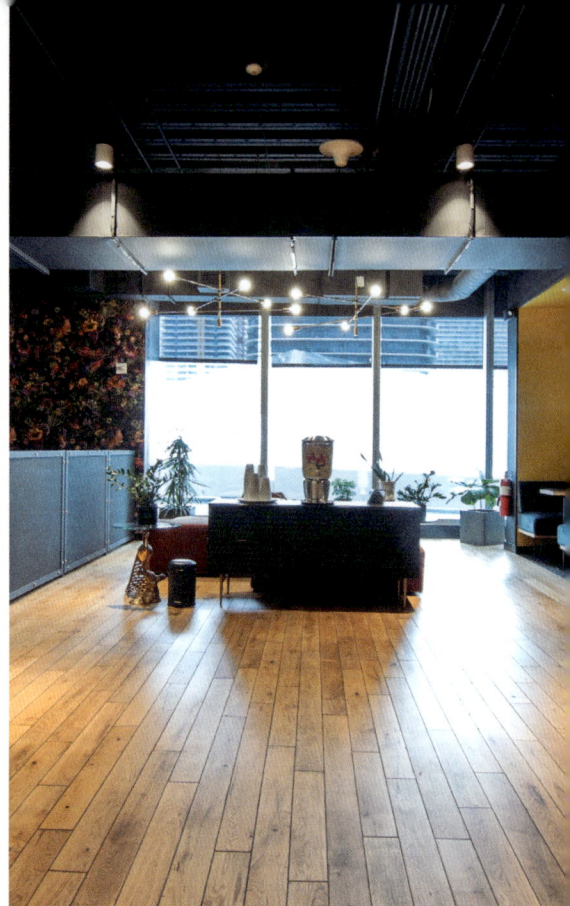

Face of the Space:

Anna Prisse is the community manager for WeWork Miami. She joined WeWork in 2015 to open up the Lincoln Road location, and now oversees operations at locations across the city. "Localizing WeWork to understanding the struggles of entrepreneurs in Miami and helping them overcome those issues and feel connected and rooted in the city while giving them the platform to expand beyond Miami is something that I'm so thrilled to be a part of," Anna says.

erts

Manny Medina
/ Cyxtera Technologies

CEO of Cyxtera

Many people in Miami are familiar with Manny Medina's name. Manny is the tech pioneer who sold his IT services company Terremark to Verizon in 2011 for $1.4 billion, and the founder and managing partner of Medina Capital Partners, a Miami-based private equity investment firm founded in 2012 that targets growth-stage companies focusing on cybersecurity, big data analytics and cloud computing. He's also the founder and chairman of the board of eMerge Americas, a platform and technology conference aiming to transform Miami, "the Magic City," into a tech hub that connects the Americas.

More recently, Medina Capital teamed up with private equity firm BC Partners to create Cyxtera Technologies, a new cybersecurity company that Manny leads as CEO. Cyxtera is the result of an acquisition deal that combined a global network of fifty-seven CenturyLink data centers with four companies (Cryptzone, Catbird, East Solutions and Brainspace) from Medina Capital's security and data analytics portfolio. At its core, Cyxtera offers a secure IT infrastructure platform to companies, governmental organizations and service providers so they can be better equipped in our ever-evolving landscape of cyber threats. With headquarters in Miami, the company currently counts over 3,500 customers and 1,300 employees. Cyxtera operates in North America, Europe, Asia and Latin America.

With more than thirty years of experience in business and technology under his belt, Manny has some wise words to share about launching a successful company in Miami. Having looked through hundreds of startup pitches received via Medina Capital, he says, "Regardless of which stage you're in, make sure you have a well-thought-out business plan that answers all the big questions in the best possible way, and be able to articulate your brand in a cohesive way. It sounds logical, but you'd be surprised how many startups just have no idea."

He also suggests demonstrating your commitment to the startup idea. "I would recommend startups to have more skin in the game," he says. "This might mean different things to different people, but the main thing is to show you're invested in the idea."

 Most important tips for startups:

- No matter what startup stage you're in, make sure
  you have a business plan that answers the important
  questions. Be thorough and articulate when writing your
  business plan. And be ready to answer the big questions
  when talking to investors or potential partners.

- Show that you're completely invested in your idea. If you're
  not demonstrating total commitment to your startup idea,
  how can you expect anyone else to be convinced by it?

- Don't be afraid to connect to members of the local startup
  community and leverage your relationships to grow your
  business. This is especially the case if you're new to Miami.
  Get out there and talk to people about your startup – it's
  easier than you think.

For entrepreneurs who are new to Miami, he tells them not be afraid to make connections with those in the local startup ecosystem and then to leverage these relationships in order to build your business. "It's easier than people think," he says. "Come here, work the market and knock on doors. If you get people on board, it makes your job a lot easier."

One way to connect with the Miami startup community and with international thought leaders is by attending the eMerge Americas annual technology conference, which Manny founded after his big Terremark-Verizon deal in order to foster the city's entrepreneurial ecosystem. The first edition debuted in 2014, and the latest edition in 2018 brought more than fifteen thousand attendees from over forty countries around the world to the sunny city. Startups attending eMerge Americas often come out of it with new contacts, knowledge and insights on how to develop their business and innovations.

In addition to Cyxtera being a sponsor for eMerge Americas, the company is engaged with various colleges and universities in Miami to provide guidance and expertise in the development of curricula in cybersecurity and other technical fields. Additionally, the company offers internship programs for students so they can get hands-on experience in this space. Though the challenges in cybersecurity are vast, Manny and his team at Cyxtera believe that there are plenty of opportunities for entrepreneurs to develop innovative solutions to protect organizations in our new age of cyber threats.

About

Cyxtera Technologies combines a worldwide footprint of best-in-class data centers with a portfolio of modern, cloud- and hybrid-ready security and analytics offerings, providing more than 3,500 enterprises, government agencies and service providers with an integrated, secure and resilient infrastructure platform for critical applications and systems. By combining a modern, hybrid-ready information security fabric with an uncommonly diverse and distributed footprint of fifty-seven world-class data centers, Cyxtera delivers a secure platform for connecting and protecting dedicated infrastructure, private clouds and public clouds.

[Contact]   Email: cyxtera.com/contact Telephone: 305-537-9500

[Links]   Web: cyxtera.com Facebook: cyxtera Twitter: @cyxtera Instagram: cyxtera

"I would recommend startups to have more skin in the game."

Jaret Davis
/ Greenberg Traurig, LLP

Comanaging Shareholder, Greenberg Traurig's Miami office

From negotiating investment deals to operating in an emerging technology sector where legislation is still unclear, dealing with legal issues is an unavoidable part of building up a startup. More often than not, founders don't have the expertise (nor the time) to navigate these critical issues. That's where legal counsel can make life easier.

"We understand the needs of entrepreneurs and early-stage investors as well as the challenges they face," says Jaret Davis, comanaging shareholder of Greenberg Traurig's Miami office. "Our emerging technologies practice is robust on both the investor and the startup side. This is critical because we know how both sides of the equation think and where the potential obstacles lie."

With company origins tracing back to 1967, Greenberg Traurig is a law firm that started in Miami and has grown to thirty-eight offices in the US, Latin America, Europe, Asia and the Middle East. Its Emerging Technologies Practice works with companies and investors at all stages, from initial business formation and angel or venture capital financing through to initial public offerings and mergers and acquisitions.

Jaret has served as comanaging shareholder of Greenberg Traurig's founding Miami office for more than a decade, and is currently a member of the firm's global executive committee. Additionally, he's worked throughout South Florida to boost and strengthen the technology ecosystem in the region. "We are incredibly proud of the role our firm has played in growing and nurturing Miami into a world-class ecosystem for technology startups," he says. Recently, Greenberg Traurig represented Medina Capital in its $3 billion joint venture with global private-equity fund BC Partners. The deal consisted of the acquisition of a portfolio of fifty-seven data centers across the globe and a suite of cybersecurity and data analytics companies, which combined to create Cyxtera Technologies.

Most important tips for startups:

- Beyond the valuation of the company and the amount being invested, there are numerous other terms that are important to investors and entrepreneurs. Terms govern the relationships between founders, the rights between entrepreneurs and investors when it comes to control of a company and much more. Terms should not be neglected nor negotiated hastily.

- Crucial to a startup company's success is the prevention of early mistakes that can be made in setting up the terms of early capitalization tables, dilution and option pools. Determining the optimal terms for stock options is necessary for long-term success and profitability.

- Get informed about exits early on, because it impacts all stages of your business. Whether it's a sale to a strategic acquirer, a private equity fund or an initial public offering (IPO), attorneys can help you form the right entity to cater to your business needs.

For emerging tech companies trying to kick-start their business, Jaret has three pieces of advice to offer. First, whether it's terms that govern the relationships between founders or terms that will be important to an investor and entrepreneur after the investment amount has been determined, be sure to ask the right questions and get legal counsel to avoid costly mistakes. No terms of any kind should be neglected or negotiated hastily.

Making a cap table is usually one of the first steps to forming a startup. Jaret believes that setting up the right terms for cap tables, dilution and option pools early on plays a big role in a startup's path to success. "Option pools, or equity offered to employees as part of compensation, are strategically important for early-stage tech startups that may not have sufficient funds to hire the requisite talent to launch a high-quality product," he explains. "As such, stock options are a powerful tool to incentivize the right talent." If you don't offer enough stock options or the terms are too onerous, your incentives might not be adequate to retain good talent. On the flip side, if you're offering too many stock options or providing terms that are too favorable to employees, your company may be less attractive to investors.

Finally, get informed about exits from the very beginning. "VC deals are always oriented toward an exit, which can take the form of a sale to a strategic acquirer, a private-equity fund or an initial public offering," Jaret says. "This exit must be properly conceptualized as it impacts all stages of the business, starting from the formation of the company." Be aware of the options you have as an end-game and what's required to achieve them; attorneys can help you form the right entity to cater to the needs of your business.

To learn more about legal topics relating to tech and entrepreneurship, check out Greenberg Traurig's LEEP (Launch, Emerge, Expand, Propel) Program, which is designed to provide legal guidance, education, mentorship and connections, or have a look at the firm's *Emerging Technology Views* blog (**gtlaw-emergingtechnologyviews.com**), which offers insights on the latest technology trends and business strategies for success.

About

Greenberg Traurig, LLP is a global, multi-practice law firm with more than two thousand attorneys serving clients from thirty-eight offices in the United States, Latin America, Europe, Asia and the Middle East. Frequently recognized for its philanthropic giving and commitment to civic involvement, Greenberg Traurig was named the largest firm in the US by Law360 in 2017, and is among the Top 20 on the *The American Lawyer* 's 2018 Global 100.

[Contact]   Web. gtlaw.com/en/contactus Telephone: 305-579-0500

[Links]   Web: gtlaw.com Facebook: GreenbergTraurigLLP Twitter: @GT_Law Instagram: gt_law

"*The exit must be properly conceptualized as it impacts all stages of the business, starting from the formation of the company.*"

Knight Foundation: Miami's Transformation Story

The Big Bet

Bold results require bold bets. It's a fact known by innovators, investors and – in our case – philanthropists.

In 2012, we made a new bet on Miami focused on entrepreneurship. We believed that investing in our city's changemakers could reap important community benefits: a stronger sense of place and possibility, increased talent retention and attraction, expanded opportunity and a greater network of engaged problem-solvers.

Miami is one of the twenty-six US cities where Knight Foundation invests, but it's also our home base, the city where we've been headquartered since 1990. Few US cities have transformed the way that Miami has in recent years, and we're proud of our role in that evolution. Since 2012, Knight has made more than two hundred investments totaling more than $25 million in entrepreneurship initiatives across Miami. This book documents much of the progress our region has made so far, and highlights the potential of what's to come. Its pages are filled with the creatives and changemakers who accelerate and embody Miami's entrepreneurial zeal.

The Journey

Rather than investing in startups directly, Knight's strategy focuses on building an entrepreneurial ecosystem. Our initial investments were rooted in three pillars:

1) **Connecting entrepreneurs at all levels:** We supported the development of idea-building spaces (such as the Idea Center at Miami Dade College and the LAB Miami, the city's first coworking center) and convenings that offer networking and learning opportunities, such as eMerge Americas and Black Tech Week.

2) **Attracting funding and mentorship:** We encouraged initiatives that connected entrepreneurs with funding opportunities, such as the Miami Angels investment group and accelerators like Endeavor Miami, the global nonprofit's first US affiliate, and 500 Startups.

3) **Building Miami's talent base:** We strengthened Miami's talent base through educational resources and programs such as LaunchCode, Girls Who Code, Babson College's Women Innovating Now Lab and Code Fever.

The common thread woven throughout has been a goal to foster a startup culture, open to the broader community, that establishes Miami as a place where ideas are built and scaled.

The Future

Our next chapter in Miami looks to build on the success of our efforts and collaborations with community members. Our next iteration of investments will focus on playing to the city's endemic attributes, namely its dynamic and diverse population, strong arts and cultural life, growth in the university system and funding potential.

We look forward to working with partners to activate the power of Miami's unique assets and provide avenues for new innovators to get involved. We're particularly focused on creating on-ramps to our ecosystem for new residents – both foreign entrepreneurs and returning Miami expats – as well as historically underrepresented communities.

Miami is a city on the rise, and we invite you to take part in the transformation.

Raul Moas
/Knight Foundation

Miami Program Director

Raul Moas, Miami program director at Knight Foundation, has played an active role in his native city's transformation from tourism hotspot to entrepreneurial hub. As managing director of Miami Angels, Florida's largest angel investor collective, Raul convened the region's best early-stage investors and startups to drive growth and long-term success.

At Knight, which focuses on fostering more informed and engaged communities, Raul is working to further grow a robust and dynamic entrepreneurial ecosystem that's accessible for all Miamians. For those looking to grow an idea or build a company, Raul has plenty of reasons why Miami is an incredible place to be. First, Miami's cultural mix offers international perspectives and opportunities. "There's a mash-up of cultures here like nowhere else, and it really fosters a global mindset from the very beginning," Raul says. "Miami is diverse, and it's this diversity that propels you to build better teams, products and companies."

Next, your dollar will go further in Miami compared to other entrepreneurial regions. "If you raise external funding, it will last you longer here because the cost to create a company is lower than in California or New York," Raul explains. To top it off, Miami is a beautiful and active community, with a recent boom in the area's arts scene. "For those who want to build a company here, they can expect not only natural beauty but also a lot of cultural and artistic activity."

For entrepreneurs hoping to launch a startup in the sunny city, Raul has some advice: Be sure you're building a product or service that you're deeply passionate about, and be sure that it solves a real need. Another thing? Go out and get connected to the community. "Immersing yourself in what's happening in town will absolutely help you build a better product. You'll encounter different ways of approaching problems that you might not have thought about otherwise." Knight funds a wide range of tech and entrepreneurial projects aimed at strengthening the Miami community. In the following pages, you'll get a snapshot of three projects the foundation has invested in – FIU Miami Urban Future Initiative, Radical Partners and Refresh Miami – and how they're making an impact in the city.

About

Knight Foundation is a national foundation with strong local roots. It invests in journalism, in the arts and in the success of cities where brothers John S. and James L. Knight once published newspapers. Its goal is to foster informed and engaged communities, which it believes are essential for a healthy democracy. The foundation has been headquartered in Miami since 1990.

[Contact] Email: moas@kf.org Telephone: 305-908-2643

[Links] Web: kf.org Facebook: knightfdn Twitter: @knightfdn Instagram: knightfdn

Still Moving
MAPPING THE STUDIO
Visual Thinking
tree houses

[Name] # Chris Caines /FIU Miami Urban Future Initiative

[Elevator Pitch] *"We're a public-private partnership between the Florida International University's CARTA (College of Communication, Architecture + the Arts) and the Creative Class Group to develop new research and insights for building a stronger and more inclusive economy in Greater Miami."*

[Sector] **Urban and economic development**

[Description] Officially launched in December 2017, the Miami Urban Future Initiative (MUFI) engages leading thinkers, researchers, business leaders and urban practitioners across the region and the world to develop research and strategies to strengthen and build a more inclusive economy in the Greater Miami area. MUFI is a joint effort between the Florida International University's College of Communication, Architecture + the Arts – where it is housed – and the Creative Glass Group, a boutique advisory firm founded by renowned urbanist Richard Florida.

Supported by funding from the John S. and James L. Knight Foundation, MUFI releases five to ten reports each year on topics related to the future of Miami's economy. It also hosts community events to drive a broader conversation about the forces shaping the city's economy. "We're assembling data, making it accessible to a wide cross section of our community, and providing context so people so can make more informed decisions," says Chris Caines, executive director of MUFI. "We're looking primarily at economic vitality and inclusion, and a large part of that is the robust nature of the startup community."

In early 2018, MUFI released a report titled "Benchmarking Miami's Innovation and Entrepreneurship" that delves into different trends and issues such as venture capital flow, the number of high-tech businesses in the region, and research and development expenditures at local universities. "Instead of just relying on anecdotal examples, our real strength is that we have a team of great researchers that can provide quantitative data on growth, opportunities and challenges for Miami as a growing startup ecosystem," says Chris. Other recent reports have examined the city's talent base and how it's dealing with globalization and affordability challenges.

[Contact] Email: **mufi@fiu.edu** Telephone: **305-535-2699**

[Links] Web: **carta.fiu.edu/mufi** Facebook: **MIAUrbanFuture** Twitter: **@MIAUrbanFuture**

[Name]

Rebecca Fishman Lipsey /Radical Partners

[Elevator Pitch]

"We're an accelerator for social impact. We scout Miami for people who are solving the issues that matter most to the future of our region and help them scale the impact of their ventures."

[Sector]

Social impact

[Description]

From housing affordability and poverty alleviation to education equity and arts and culture, Radical Partners supports startups and leaders tackling issues that will play a key role in shaping the future of the Miami region. "We spend half of our time mobilizing different sources of power to invest in solutions locally and the other half on helping leaders scale," explains Rebecca Fishman Lipsey, who founded Radical Partners in 2012 when Miami was emerging as a startup city.

Radical Partners' signature program is the Social Entrepreneurship Bootcamp, a three-month accelerator program that helps a cohort of ten to twelve innovators develop and scale their ventures each year. The bootcamp helps accelerate the impact of selected ventures through intensive workshops, networking events and tailored coaching sessions, as well as access to industry experts and mentors that are well versed in areas that matter to growing social impact projects. Since its launch, four cohorts have gone through the program, including projects such as Nu Deco Ensemble ("a virtuosic and eclectic chamber orchestra designed for the twenty-first century") and Melanites (a "toy company that creates diverse toys, storybooks and games that celebrate brown boyhood and inspire children of color to dream big"). In addition to the bootcamp, Radical Partners runs a Leadership Lab which supports grassroots leaders working on initiatives that strengthen their neighborhoods. This program consists of an eight-week intensive fellowship on nights and weekends and provides access to a variety of resources, tools, coaching and mentors.

When looking at the future of Miami's innovation ecosystem, Rebecca says the next chapter is about scaling. "In a really powerful and rapid way, Miami has gone down the road of becoming a startup city, much to Knight Foundation's credit," she says. "We're seeing a lot of ventures that have launched and are doing meaningful work.... Our focus now is shifting from launching to scaling."

[Contact]   Email: info@radicalpartners.net Telephone: 305-535-2699

[Links]   Web: radical.partners Facebook: radicalpartners Twitter: @RadicalPartners

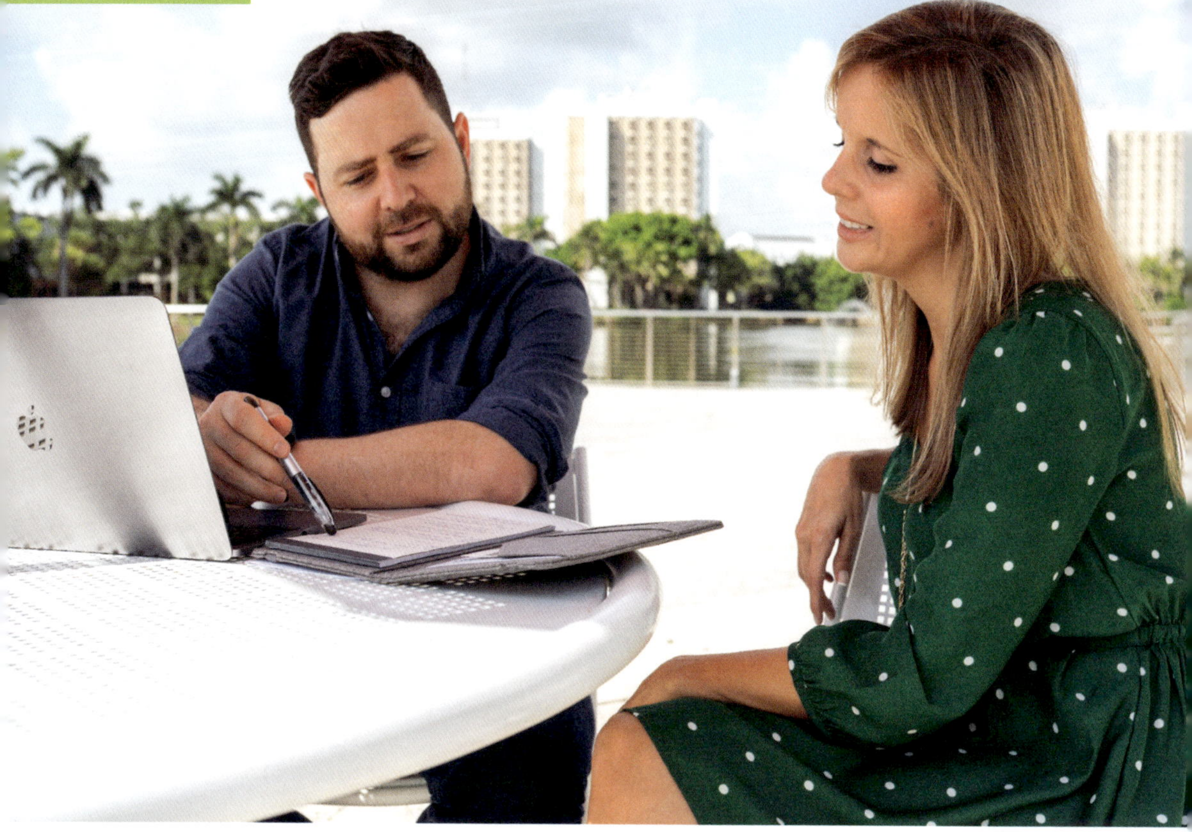

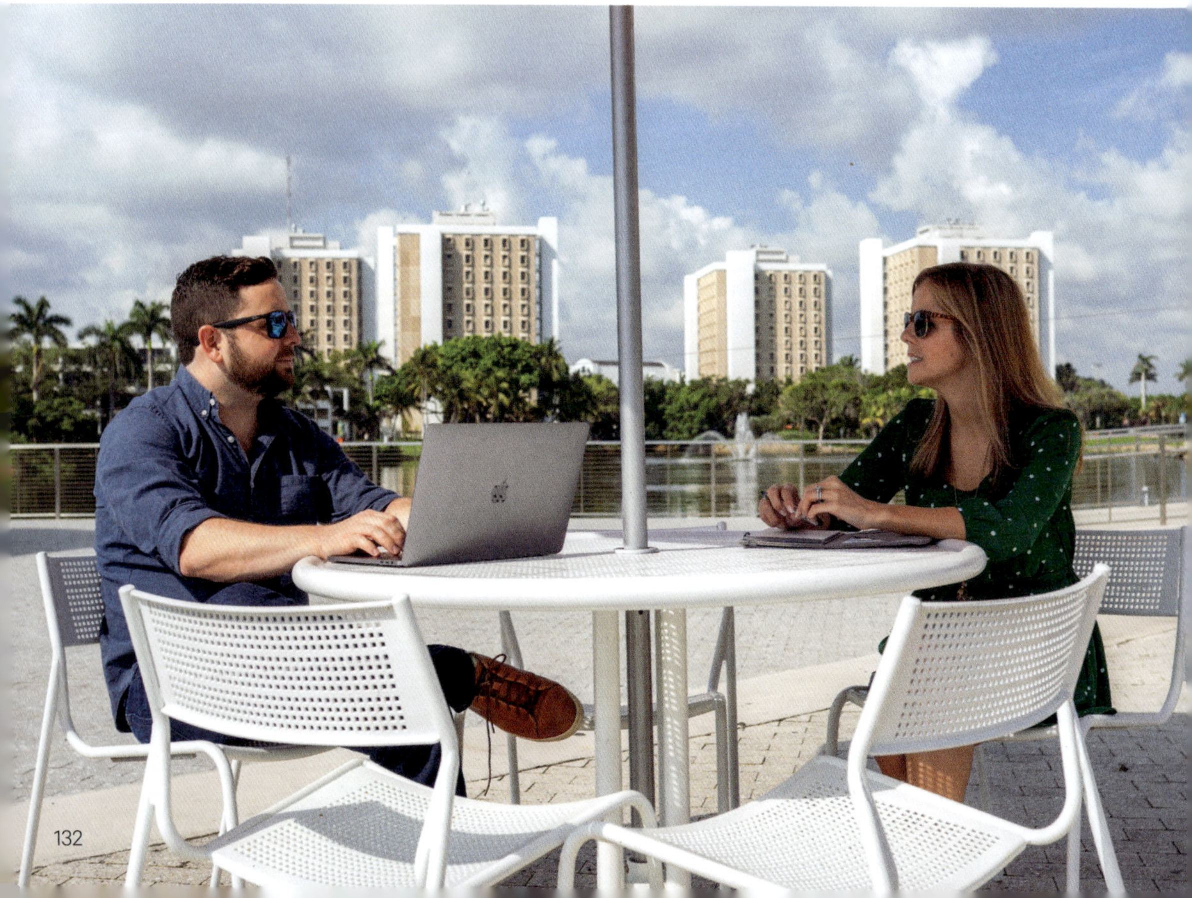

[Name]

Maria Derchi
/Refresh Miami

[Elevator Pitch]

"Our mission is to educate, inspire, connect and grow South Florida's tech and startup community."

[Sector]

Community Building

[Description]

"Refresh is a byproduct of entrepreneurs wanting to connect with each other and share ideas in South Florida," says Maria Derchi, who serves as Refresh Miami's executive director. "We've been able to grow organically because of the thirst for this type of knowledge-sharing, professional growth and development and community-building." Refresh was born twelve years ago, when Brian Breslin moved back to his hometown of Miami after college and began looking for an opportunity to network and learn from tech professionals. When his research came up short, he rallied five people via Meetup.com to a local Starbucks and formed Refresh Miami. Now Refresh Miami boasts over ten thousand members and is the largest tech and entrepreneurial community in Florida.

At Refresh's speaker events, which average between two hundred and three hundred attendees each month, entrepreneurs have the opportunity to learn from industry heavyweights such as Alexis Ohanian, cofounder of Reddit; Jim Mckelvey, cofounder of Square; and Jason Calacanis, prominent angel investor, entrepreneur and author – just to name a few. Refresh also offers skill-building workshops on topics such as how to pitch investors, search-engine optimization, bot framework, public relations and media training. Refresh also encourages entrepreneurs to connect and collaborate through attendance at its quarterly networking events.

Beyond its in-person events, Refresh maintains a community-sourced website and email newsletter, keeping its members informed of the latest in Miami tech and startup news, job opportunities, events, accelerator applications, funding sources and more. "It's about more than just us; it's about growing and supporting the community as a whole," Maria says. "After over a decade of this work, our focus has not changed and we remain as committed as ever to our goal." Base membership in Refresh Miami is free. There are two additional paid membership tiers that allow access to exclusive perks such as speaker dinners, discounts on workshops and more.

[Apply to]

Web: refreshmiami.com/contact

[Links]

Web: refreshmiami.com Facebook: refreshmiami Twitter: @refreshmiami

Ken Russell / Miami Downtown Development Authority

Chairman of Miami Downtown Development Authority and City of Miami District 2 Commissioner

When most people think about Miami, images of sun, fun and the beach spring to mind, but those are not the only advantages of doing business in the Magic City. Increasingly, companies, entrepreneurs and creatives are drawn to Miami for its diverse population, high quality of life, proximity to Latin America and strong economy.

Case in point: 500 Startups, the well-known Silicon Valley-based venture capital fund and seed accelerator, opened a 7,200 ft^2 office in the heart of Downtown Miami earlier this year with support from the Miami Downtown Development Authority (Miami DDA), Knight Foundation and Visa. Since launching operations, 500 Startups has brought its world-class resources, expertise and investors to Miami's entrepreneurial community, including the fund's signature ten-week Road to Series A program.

While attracting big names in tech is important to the city (Miami also nabbed a spot on Amazon's shortlist for its second headquarters), the top priority for local officials and agencies like the Miami DDA is to support the growth of the city's urban core neighborhoods and ensure they remain a vibrant and desirable place to live, work and visit.

Ken Russell, an entrepreneur-turned-politician and currently the chairman of the Miami DDA and the City of Miami District 2 Commissioner, has some advice for anyone considering Miami as a base to launch a startup or scale a company: First and foremost, don't take common assumptions about Miami at face value. "There's so much more going for Miami than sun and sand – that's not what brings companies to the city. Companies are looking for a place that's on the rise, not one that's already exhausted or overbuilt. If you do your research on Miami, you'll see that there's a lot of opportunity here."

Second, make sure to network – in real life. It's easy to go online and find out who's doing what, but this rarely provides a complete picture of what's happening on the ground in the startup community. "Build relationships locally to test the waters and see if there's a good fit for your company," he says. "Whether it's through the City of Miami, the Miami DDA or otherwise, there are many ways to get involved in the startup scene and meet potential partners. The first step is to reach out and let us help."

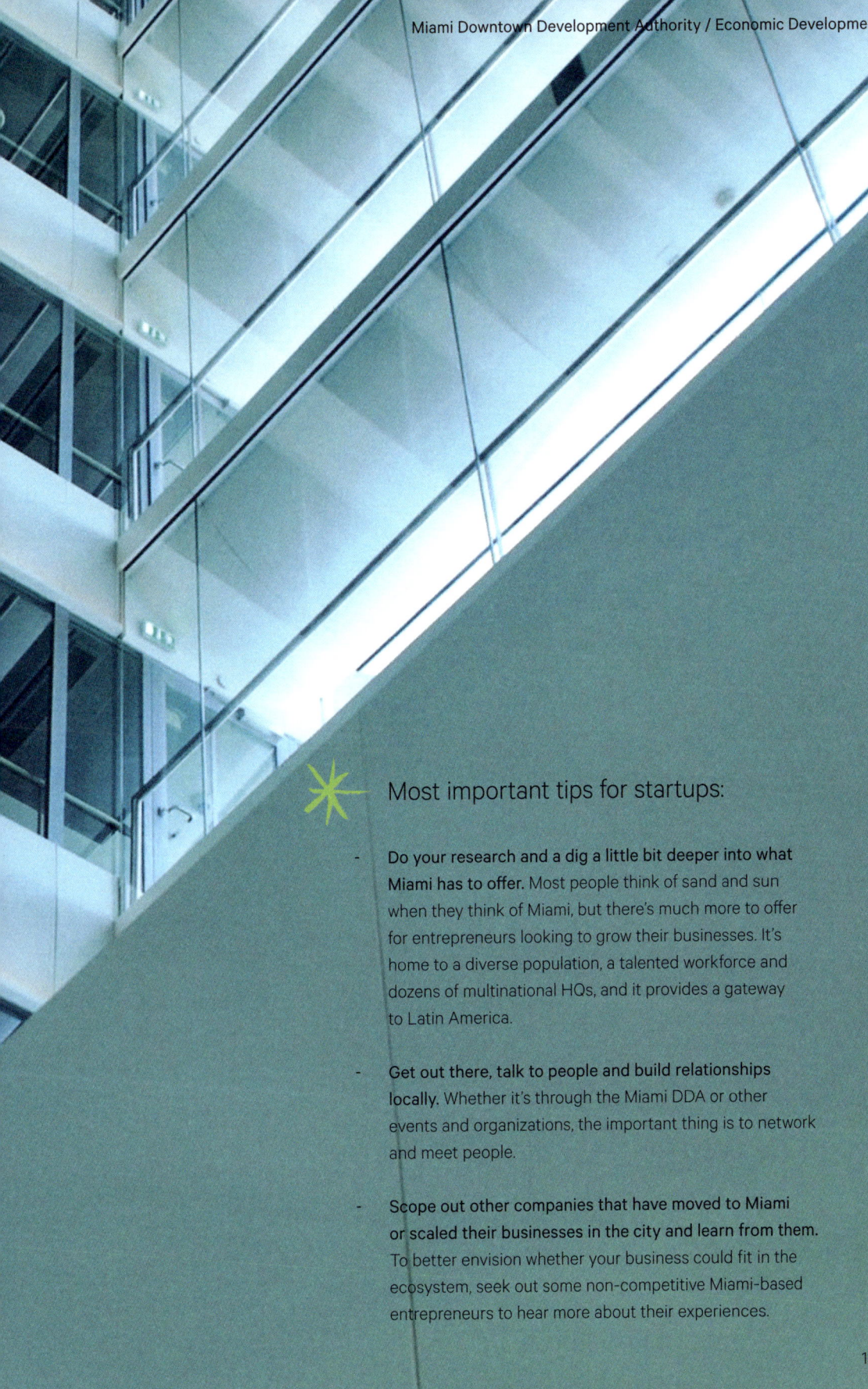

Most important tips for startups:

- Do your research and a dig a little bit deeper into what Miami has to offer. Most people think of sand and sun when they think of Miami, but there's much more to offer for entrepreneurs looking to grow their businesses. It's home to a diverse population, a talented workforce and dozens of multinational HQs, and it provides a gateway to Latin America.

- Get out there, talk to people and build relationships locally. Whether it's through the Miami DDA or other events and organizations, the important thing is to network and meet people.

- Scope out other companies that have moved to Miami or scaled their businesses in the city and learn from them. To better envision whether your business could fit in the ecosystem, seek out some non-competitive Miami-based entrepreneurs to hear more about their experiences.

Another way to gain insight on whether your startup or business might be a good fit for Miami's tech ecosystem is by reaching out to companies that have decided to move to Miami or scale in the city. "There are many non-competitive partners from different sectors that can tell you what they've been through and the pluses and minuses of choosing Miami as a home for their company," he says. "I'm confident they'll give a good report card."

More than ninety thousand people now call Downtown Miami home, a number that is expected to grow by twenty thousand over the next three years. According to a recent report by the Miami DDA, people between the ages of twenty-five and forty-four make up the bulk of Downtown's residential population, and the area is home to more than 175,000 jobs, cementing its position as the entrepreneurial and economic engine of the city.

In addition to encouraging business development and leading the charge for pedestrian-friendly streets and more arts and cultural amenities, the Miami DDA actively engages with tech startups and other businesses to learn about the opportunities and challenges they face. The agency has created financial incentives and – through its business concierge service – helps entrepreneurs navigate the process of setting up a business in Miami, from permits to finding office space.

"I believe Miami is a template for the rest of the country, and the world. We're much further ahead in terms of a diverse workforce that embraces different cultures and languages," says Ken. "Miami has long been viewed as a gateway between Europe and South America, and the companies that come here are ones that embrace new ideas and want that global perspective."

About

The Miami Downtown Development Authority (Miami DDA) is an independent agency of the City of Miami funded by a special tax levy on properties within its district boundaries. The agency is governed by a fifteen-member board of directors, which includes three public appointees and twelve downtown property owners, business owners and residents. The board sets policy direction, which is implemented by a multidisciplinary team under the oversight of the executive director. Its mission is to grow, strengthen and promote the economic health and vitality of Downtown Miami.

"*Build relationships locally to test the waters and see if there's a good fit for your company.*"

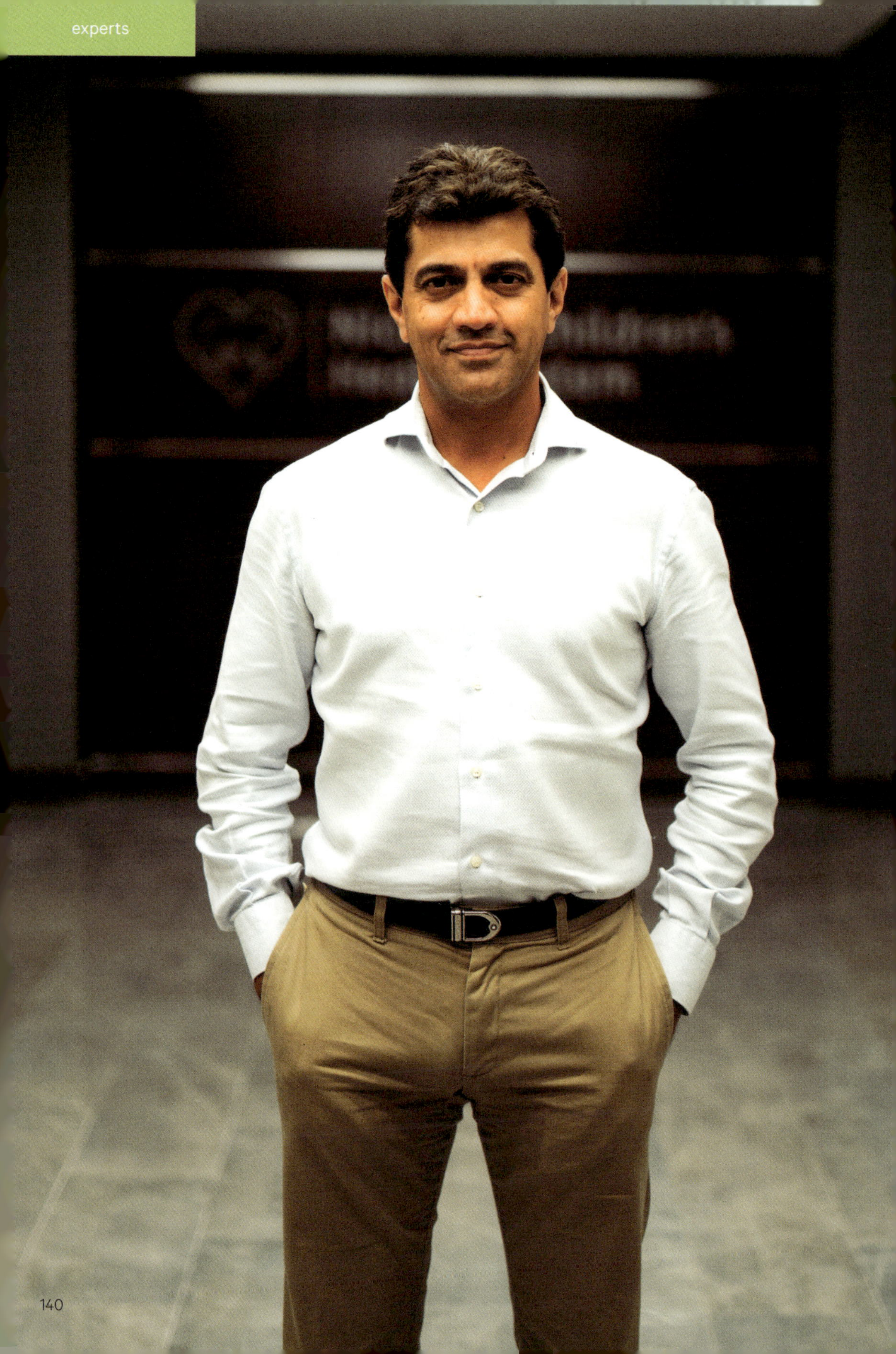

Dr. Narendra Kini / Nicklaus Children's Health System

CEO at Nicklaus Children's Health System

Digital health is booming, and the healthcare industry is still ripe for disruption. According to data from Crunchbase, venture funding for US biotech and healthcare startups reached $14.5 billion in 2017. To all the health-tech startups: What are you waiting for? Now is the time to get your innovative idea out there and try to make a difference. The future of healthcare is in your hands.

Nicklaus Children's Health System is well aware of the potential for tech innovations to revamp different areas in the health industry. That's why it was one of the first healthcare systems to create a for-profit venture arm – Children's Health Ventures – to support and partner with startups working in this realm with investment, mentorship and a platform to test their ideas. "Essentially, we offer up our health system as a living laboratory where entrepreneurs can bring in a raw idea, even if it's in the pre-commercialization phase," says Dr. Narendra Kini, CEO of Nicklaus Children's Health System. "We allow them to interact with patients, families, doctors and others in the health ecosystem to test the idea. And we're willing to co-develop the idea with them and provide mentorship as well as enable them to get other rounds of financing." Children's Health Ventures has invested in six startups so far.

To make it easier for entrepreneurs considering health tech, Narendra has shared his top pieces of advice about starting up in this sector. "The first thing is to understand the problem you're solving in healthcare and who the customer is," he says. "Is your customer the patient, the family, the doctor, the insurance company or the health system? Know exactly what you want to achieve with your idea."

From getting an in-depth understanding of the health ecosystem and patient privacy to integrating with existing systems and navigating complex regulations, there's no doubt that building a health-tech startup comes with its own set of challenges. That's why Narendra highly recommends you get a mentor on board as soon as possible. "A healthcare mentor can help advocate for your idea, de-risk it by spotting gaps that most entrepreneurs may not pick up on and guide you in navigating entities like the FDA," he says. On that note, it also doesn't hurt to bring on angel investors who are well versed in the healthcare industry. One thing's for sure: If entrepreneurs are able to overcome the obstacles and gain traction for their product or service, this path can be incredibly rewarding and leave an impact on many people's lives.

Most important tips for startups:

- **Understand the problem you're trying to solve and who you're trying to target as a customer.** Is your digital health product or service for patients, families, doctors, insurance companies or the healthcare systems? What exactly are you trying to achieve? You should be able to answer these questions.

- **Look for a mentor in the healthcare sector as early as you can.** An experienced mentor can help advocate for your idea, offer insights on any gaps in your product or service, and support you in navigating entities like the FDA.

- **Don't forget about intellectual property.** There are a million and one things to do as a health-tech entrepreneur, but it's critical that you don't forget about protecting your intellectual property. Neglecting it could have serious consequences to the valuation of your company in the future.

In the midst of all the tasks that come with building up a health-tech startup, it's easy to forget about intellectual property. Don't, because it could mean losing a lot of your overall valuation as a company down the line, says Narendra. "At the end of the day, startups can do well, but if they don't remember to protect their intellectual property by patenting it, copyrighting it or trademarking it, there could be serious implications in the future." Considering how competitive the digital health space is becoming, it's certainly a critical aspect to think about early on.

Looking to the next decade, Narendra believes that Miami will soon become the world center for digital health innovation. "There's a core cluster of healthcare systems with enough clinical workflow and technology available for entrepreneurs to try their ideas on," he says, "and its proximity to Latin America means there's an incredible opportunity to build digital healthcare products for one of the fastest-growing populations in the United States. There are enormous opportunities."

About

Nicklaus Children's Health System is the region's only healthcare system exclusively for children. It includes the organization's flagship, Nicklaus Children's Hospital; a network of outpatient centers, as well as Nicklaus Children's Hospital Foundation, the organization's fundraising arm; Pediatric Specialists of America Inc., a nonprofit physician practice subsidiary; a management services organization; an ambulatory surgery center; and KidzStuff™, an ecommerce line of children's wellness and safety products that support the hospital's mission of serving the region's pediatric population.

" Startups can do well, but if they don't remember to protect their intellectual property by patenting it, copyrighting it or trademarking it, there could be serious implications in the future. "

Ann Rosenberg
/ SAP Next-Gen

Senior Vice President and Global Head of SAP Next-Gen

These days it's no longer enough for companies and startups to run a profitable business; it's also about having purpose and valuing social responsibility. "More and more investors and corporations are asking startups about the social impact of their products or services," says Ann Rosenberg, senior vice president and global head of SAP Next-Gen. "Building a purpose-driven startup is becoming a normality."

Still, there's a common misconception that "social businesses" means "organizations that don't make a profit." Ann believes that earning money can, indeed, be compatible with building solutions that make a difference in the world. "Being purpose-driven is more about how your product or service is leaving a positive contribution to society and how you reinvest what's earned, rather than whether you're earning money," she says. "Of course, startups should make a profit in order to scale and accelerate their businesses."

For the budding entrepreneur who has an exciting idea tackling one of the world's most pressing challenges but who doesn't know how to get it off the ground, Ann suggests submitting it to a crowdsourcing platform for starters. Nowadays there's a variety of platforms that offer emerging innovators the support, the resources and the access to a network of mentors they need to help them accelerate their ideas and impact. SAP Next-Gen is teaming up with a number of accelerators and corporations and has just launched the SDG Accelerator in partnership with Global Startup Ecosystem.

"By crowdsourcing the embedded knowledge of a global community of startups, accelerators, corporates, purpose-driven institutions, academia and citizens, we can rapidly uncover new solutions to address the United Nations Global Goals," says Ann. Often referred to "Innovation 3.0," this kind of collective collaboration across disciplines, organizations and communities allows innovators and entrepreneurs to leverage the vast knowledge that our dynamic digital landscape offers in order to propel their socially conscious ideas forward more effectively.

Most important tips for startups:

- **Ensure your startup idea is linked to the United Nations 17 Global Goals.** Now more than ever, startups and entrepreneurs need to think about how they will leave a positive contribution to society. One way to do this is to tie your product or service into one of the UN 17 Global Goals.

- **Submit your purpose-driven idea to a crowdsourcing platform to help get it noticed.** Crowdsourcing platforms can help innovators tap into the embedded knowledge of a global community of startups, accelerators, corporates, purpose-driven institutions, academia and citizens to propel ideas forward.

- **Tailor your pitch so you can clearly communicate your mission to different audiences that can help you achieve greater impact.** For early-stage entrepreneurs trying to kickstart their purpose-driven business, collaborating with experts, bigger industry players and more established organizations can lead to growth and more impactful innovation.

In 2015, world leaders outlined the UN 17 Global Goals for sustainable development with the aim of creating a better future by 2030. They include eradicating poverty, eliminating hunger, achieving gender equality, offering better education and providing clean water for all, among others. Since then, Ann says these goals have been quickly adopted and have become guideposts for entrepreneurs, organizations and governments. One way to ensure your business is connected to social good is by linking it to one of these ambitious goals, which SAP Next-Gen is committed to supporting. Ann suggests entrepreneurs learn about the UN Sustainable Development Goals at globalgoals.org/business.

Once you've understood the 17 Global Goals and tied your startup's solution to one of them, it's about being able to clearly communicate your mission and vision to different kinds of audiences such as corporations, VCs and potential collaborators. Remember that you'll have to tailor the language and approach of your pitch depending on who you're talking to and what their needs are. Leading a purpose-driven business isn't easy, and finding ways to collaborate with experts, bigger industry players and established organizations can fuel growth and expand your impact.

In Miami, social entrepreneurship is a realm that's certainly heating up. Not only that, the sunny city's unique geographic location has made it a hot hub for startups from Latin America. "What's special about Miami is that it's a bridge that connects the innovation ecosystems in Latin America with the US," says Ann.

About

SAP Next-Gen is a purpose-driven innovation university and community aligned with SAP's commitment to the 17 UN Global Goals for sustainable development. The community leverages 3,600+ educational institutions in 116 countries, 110+ SAP Next-Gen labs/hubs at universities and at partner and SAP locations and nearly 100 SAP Next-Gen Chapters, as well as entrepreneurs, accelerators, tech community partners, venture firms, futurists and purpose-driven institutions.

SAP Next-Gen connects companies around the world to academic thought leaders and researchers, students, startups, accelerators, tech community partners, purpose-driven partners, venture firms, futurists and SAP experts to reimagine the future of industries and intelligent enterprise; seed in disruptive innovation with startups; build skills for digital futures; and use new mindsets such as science fiction thinking and initiatives such as #sheinnovates to accelerate "Innovation with Purpose" linked to the SDGs.

[Contact]   email: ann.rosenberg@sap.com

[Links]   Web: sap.com/next-gen Facebook: SAPNextGen Twitter: @SAPNextGen Instagram: sapnextgen

"Ensure your startup idea is linked to the United Nations seventeen Global Goals. Now more than ever, startups and entrepreneurs need to think about how they will leave a positive contribution to society."

foun

ders

Felecia Hatcher

Executive Director and Founder / Code Fever, BlackTech Week,
Space Called Tribe

A scholarship service, a gourmet popsicle company, an annual landmark conference
and national tour for Black entrepreneurs, a coding school for minorities, a coworking
space in the heart of Miami's historic Overtown: Felecia Hatcher's path has been anything
but ordinary. Now she is at the forefront of a local South Florida movement to bring diversity
to tech, an industry notorious for its homogeneity.

What was your entrepreneurial path?
I started my first business in college. It was called Urban Excellence, an educational
consulting company. A friend of mine, James Taylor, and I started it after I won $130,000 in
scholarships and grants as C-students in high school, and he won a full ride sports scholarship.
Organizations and major companies would hire us to develop scholarship and college-prep
training programs for high school students. We worked with individual families as well to help
their students find scholarships and get into the college of their choice when their grades
weren't that great.

I ran a very short-lived PR company and also worked in marketing for some tech companies like
Sony and Nintendo, Wells Fargo, Second Life video games, and McKee Foods, which produces
Little Debbie snack cakes, as well as the NBA. Then in 2008 when the economy crashed, I left
corporate America for good to start Feverish Pops.

My husband Derick and I ran a gourmet popsicle manufacturing company for seven years here
in Miami. We had a bunch of corporate clients, so Google, PayPal, Forever 21, Airbnb, Capitol
Records, etc. We'd manufacture gourmet ice pops for them and ran a store too. Most of our
business centered around private label manufacturing and shipping nationwide. Then we got
VC funding to expand what we were doing.

With Feverish, we had a social mission, so a portion of every ice pop we sold went to funding
something in the community that we were passionate about. A lot of it went to creating a
program called PopPrenuers where we showed kids how to run their own popsicle business.
We tackled youth unemployability with our program from a social standpoint, running it as a
part of Feverish for about two or three years.

How did the idea for your company come about?

Diverse ecosystems are really important, so we started doing ecosystem building work specifically around making sure that the Black community was fully engaged in everything that was going on in Miami's Innovation economy. We started off with monthly tech panels, just kinda bringing together diverse people who were working in tech and entrepreneurship in Miami and having conversations about sharing resources and what was going on. And then we started BlackTech Week to dive deeper into building asset- and talent-filled spaces in Black communities by drawing resources, training, networks, funding, and inclusive policies into Black communities, so that these communities would be valued as massive assets within the innovation sector. And so that, no matter if you're a young person, a beginning startup founder, someone more established in the tech field as a professional, or someone launching or growing a tech company, you could get all the resources you needed during that one week and our national tour stops. So that's what we set out to do. Michael Seibel (the CEO of Y Combinator), John Lewis Jr. (the chief diversity officer for Coca Cola) and Bobby Seale (one of the founders of the original Black Panther Party) were some of the keynote speakers over the years. Our work is about ridding Black communities of innovation deserts. Black and brown communities are being completely disconnected from the innovation economy and most importantly from the financial benefits.

What early struggles did you have, and how did you overcome them while starting out?

A lot of people did not understanding the importance of diversifying startup ecosystems, and that came from both sides: inside the community we serve as well as outside of it. People just did not fully understand that there actually is an issue and a disconnect, and that race is playing a huge role in that. We have had many amazing partners now – Knight Foundation, Comcast, Ford Foundation, Simkins Family Foundation, Chan Zuckerberg Initiative – but in the beginning, raising the funding to actually continue to do this work and to transition to doing the work full time, because it just required that, that was an issue. Another was being able to hold more of the organizations committed to supporting the entrepreneur ecosystem in Miami and across the US accountable and making sure that they fully understood that they weren't being diverse or inclusive in their efforts. It took work to create a lot of content around changing the narrative of where we think innovation happens and who we think is an innovator.

And then there were the everyday challenges of just trying to build an organization internally as well: the funding, developing trainings and curriculums, putting stakeholders together, building a team – all of that has been a challenge.

" *Our work is about ridding black communities of innovation deserts. Black and brown communities are being completely disconnected from the innovation economy.* "

What was your biggest mistake?

Let's see, the biggest mistake... there were so many. So many. There were big ones getting Code Fever and BlackTech Week off the ground, not giving ourselves enough time to promote, especially in year one of the conference. That was a really big one. Putting together a really good team, a dedicated team, was hard in the very beginning, and so that was something we struggled with getting right. I mean, it's still a struggle. Personality dynamics, getting the culture right, these things are always a struggle, but it was bigger in the early days of just trying to figure out how to make that work. A Space Called Tribe, our coworking space, took two years to get open, so there were a lot there too.

What was your best decision?

There are a lot of good ones, too. I think our best decision was starting BlackTech Week. Starting Code Fever was a great decision, but BlackTech Week was the best because it did everything we needed it to do, and it continues to do that. It's more than a conference; by bringing people here, whether they were speakers or conference attendees, it also allowed us to shine a light on Miami and tell a story of the innovators and opportunities that exist here. You know that most people just don't think that people work in Miami? There's also a perception that Black people don't really exist in Miami, which is wild because they represent almost 20 percent of the population here, and that's a problem. Miami's just deemed as a party city, right? Like, you come to party, you come for vacation, but you don't actually come to work and build companies. And then when you talk about the people who actually work, it's not a layered story like it should be. And so the conference, more than being a resource, has also been one of the biggest storytellers of not only the Black experience but the unique cultural experience that exists here, with so many cultures coming together: the Latin American culture, the Caribbean culture, White American, Black American; it just all comes together. And so this, for me, is why that was one of the best decisions. A number of entrepreneurs who have been able to raise money from being a part of BlackTech Week go on to get accepted into Techstars, 500 and other accelerators. Getting youth exposure to great minds, professionals getting positions with companies, and building startups, all of that has made it the best business.

What do you wish you'd known before you started, and what would you have done differently?

The most honest answer is, if I'd have known how hard and crazy it would be to put on an annual conference and do the work at the magnitude of what we've done, I don't know if I'd have done it. Just to be honest, right? It's a lot, and it takes a big emotional and personal toll, even with all the success we've had. It's just kind of the nature of everything that we've done. So if I'd have known that, I may not have continued to go down that road or pursued the idea. And I would relate that answer to starting Space Called Tribe – the amount of time and work that it took to get the building going, to continue to fill it and support entrepreneurs, and even be in a city that's so, so underestimated... it's a lot to carry.

What professional advice would you give people in the early stages of starting out?

I saw a meme last week and saved it: it was like, "Your failure to ask for help is a trauma response," and I can believe that. It's kinda frowned upon to ask for help. It's seen as being weak, and not as being resourceful. So build an advisory board very early. I think so often it's kinda left to nonprofits, startups or companies to put together an advisory board. Because you just need the help. Too often people wait too long to seek out the help they need.

And what do you like about working in Miami?

The people. I travel a lot, so I get to interface with not just people across the United States but even internationally, and Miami people are really unique. I don't even know like how to describe it. We just have our own way of doing everything, and it's just really fun – it's beautiful. I mean, it may not always be the best, but I wouldn't trade it for the world. If you were to ask me seven years ago, I would have told you I can't wait to get the hell out of Miami, because everything else was so much shinier. But it's turned into a really cool city, and it's one of those places where it's not oversaturated. Miami is one of those places where you can come and start something, and people aren't really gonna stand in your way. You don't have too many gatekeepers that won't allow you to do things or at least try.

[About]   BlackTech Week founder Felecia Hatcher also runs Code Fever, a nonprofit that teaches tech skills; and Space Called Tribe, a coworking space located in Miami's historic Overtown neighborhood. She and her husband Derick Pearson are linchpins of the Miami tech ecosystem and their work focuses on diversity and community.

[Links]   Web: blacktechweek.com Facebook: BlackTechWeek Twitter: @BlackTechWeek

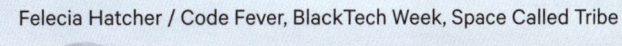

What are your top work essentials?
My iPhone, my Bose noise-canceling headphones
and my laptop, absolutely!

At what age did you found your company?
Thirty.

What's your most-used app?
Probably Slack.

**What's the most valuable piece of advice
you've been given?**
Follow your most epic dreams.

What's your greatest skill?
Probably being a communicator and storyteller.

Guido Kovalskys

Cofounder and CEO of Nearpod

Buenos Aires native Guido Kovalskys is cofounder and CEO of Nearpod, an online classroom tool that helps teachers engage students with interactive lessons. Founded in 2012, the company now has one hundred and twenty employees, multiple millions in revenue and contracts with school districts across the country. A graduate of UC Berkley's Haas school of Business and a Mackenzie alum, Guido is a serial entrepreneur whose past successes include Bionexo, a business that develops digital solutions for hospital supply chains across Latin America.

What was your entrepreneurial path?

I went to UC Berkeley grad school in the days of the early dot-com boom, so even though I was on the conservative path of consulting, the reality of California and the fact that anybody who had a really good idea could bring it to market was really a rocking concept for me. In my country, you'd be starting a restaurant or a small shop. In California, you could have really bold ideas that people would actually back, even though they seemed risky. That, to me, was a whole new experience, and I was amazed. And of course, it seemed very appealing to me. At the same time, I had my student loans, but after a couple of years I decided I couldn't shy away from my calling anymore. So I went down to Latin America and started not only Bionexo but also another series of ventures. It was mostly an umbrella company – what today would be called an incubator – but that didn't exist back then. That was a very exciting path.

How did the idea for the company come about?

Education had always been an interest to me, and I'd seen the potential and the power of using technology to alter educational outcomes. But if you go into a classroom today, it doesn't really look any different from past classrooms. The kids get their information through those lectures or through text books, and then they do some sort of paper-based assessment that the teacher uses for grading, giving feedback and helping them understand who is doing an adequate job.

We felt like that was a very unkind model, and we thought that with the one-to-one revolution, every student would be able to have an internet-connected device in their hands during instructional time. That was going to be a game-changer for how instruction happens.

What early struggles did you guys have, and how did you overcome them while starting out?
Needless to say, funding wasn't easy. It was the combination of not being in Silicon Valley, and the focus on education and K-12, and the fact that for Silicon Valley standards we weren't proven entrepreneurs; because in the Valley, anything that you've done outside the Valley really doesn't count much. All that made it really tough for us to get funding. We overcame that by being super lean and bootstrapping as much as we could, meaning we self-funded the startup. Then, when we had some meaningful traction, I decided to move things forward to the Bay Area to get our fundraising motion going, which happened. Once the company had its own merits and multiple millions in revenues and contracts with schools and districts, we felt that we needed to have everyone in the team in the same office, and so we decided to relocate the company to Miami. At the beginning, it was a combination of bootstrapping, being super lean and going really, really slowly. Then we got some early funds from an excellent group of investors from Silicon Valley, and once people saw that, several local South Florida venture funds got really excited about what we were doing and decided to invest as well.

What was your biggest mistake?
I'd say that we took a bit too long to focus. We were flailing too much at the beginning. We thought that the technology also had higher education potential and that eventually we could use it for colleges and universities, and we kind of tried to do both. That probably distracted us over the first two or three years. But the only reason we were hedging our bets was because the narrative around doing business in K-12 was so negative. Everybody warned us that this wasn't going to work, that K-12 and school districts take forever to buy, that they spend most of their funds on print textbooks and that the teachers are really slow adopters of technology. The naysayers really warned us to avoid the space, but our gut feeling was, "Wait a minute, I think we are at a point of inflection."

❝ *You never get the right to play in the next league unless you're very successful in the early days.* **❞**

What was your best decision?

Once we had enough data points to know that K-12 had a lot of potential, we were early movers. Administrators and districts realized that they can't teach a student in analog ways when the life of the students and the jobs they're going to have going forward are digital. And I think we were super early in betting on that. So, that's one. The other was that when we started fundraising, we didn't get carried away by the temptation to just focus on building a large user base and figure out monetization later. We had a conviction that it was extremely important to prove that our company could be self-sustainable, so as much effort as we put into discovering a product/market fit we also put into figuring out a way to monetize the product we were developing.

So, there were two decisions: first, we saw the trend early and went after it; and, second, we didn't get carried away by figuring out product and engagement now and monetizing later. We had to actually spend a lot of time thinking about how to monetize what we were building.

What do you wish you'd known before you started, and what would you have done differently?

We waited too long to bring the next generation of management. We waited almost four or five years, and I think bringing in some expertise earlier would have been a good call. We over-relied on our founder intuition and energy, but we could have used the help of people who had been there, done that before. The company will be about 150 people by the end of the year. We have a really strong management team that we hired over the last twelve to eighteen months, and the day-to-day requires a lot less of our presence. But I'd say we don't regret too many things. We are quite happy with the journey.

What professional advice would you give people in the early stages of starting out?

Be super lean. It's interesting, because people need to think big picture and think about how to change the world, etc., but your early challenge has nothing to do with the big picture, right?

Your only challenges are, How do I get my first couple of users to pay and renew? How do I make sure they're extremely happy? How do I solve some really nasty bugs affecting my whole product? The early days are so much about the details. You need to be super obsessive, super lean, super in-the-day, today. You also need to be able to talk and sell the big picture, but that's only about 15 percent of your job. Some people get so carried away by the "I'm changing the world" thing that they forget that the only way to buy a ticket to that game is by doing the early, early, early steps, which are the minutiae. So, that's my biggest one. The second one is, if you're going to get into this crazy thing of entrepreneurship, you need to be stubborn. The number of people who will say "no" to your sales pitch early on, to your fundraising pitch, when you've tried to recruit people – you know, that can be a little depressing. And some nights, you go back and say, Why am I doing all this? This is just so uphill? But knowing that the journey will be more losses than wins is a good thing, because there are a lot of people who think it's all fun and exciting fundraising and showing "vanity" metrics, but the day-to-day is just grueling. So, my second advice is, know what you're getting into.

All right, and what do you like about working in Miami?
It's a great place to start companies. It's a place where young people want to live. It's a place where you can go by the model of "work hard, play hard." It's very cosmopolitan, which brings a lot of diversity to your team. Even though it's not the cheapest place on the planet, it's a lot more affordable than New York, San Francisco, Boston, etc., for office space, for housing. It's also close to everywhere. It's close to Latin America, Europe, the East Coast. Plus the education market in Miami is so strong. I mean, we have two of the largest school districts in the country, Broward and Miami-Dade, and that's a luxury. There's also an expansive network of private independent schools that we can work with. So, there's a bunch of things to like about Miami as opposed to New York, San Francisco or Boston. Probably the biggest challenge for us is the shortage of tech talent. Unfortunately, most technical folks end up moving to bigger tech markets due to lack of great job opportunities locally, But we're obviously trying to change that by fostering the local tech ecosystem. For me, personally, I'm a flight away from my family in South America, so that's something I really appreciate.

[About]   **Nearpod** publishes an interactive tool that helps teachers engage students with digital lessons. The company focuses on the K-12 age range and generates revenue from membership plans and from an online marketplace for lessons.

What are your top work essentials?
Exercise before going to work.

At what age did you found your company?
This one at age forty-two.

What's your most-used app?
Gmail, by far.

What's the most valuable piece of advice you've been given?
Your biggest asset is your personal reputation, your personal brand.

What's your greatest skill?
Attitude. Positivity. Looking forward. That's contagious. People like to work with people that are positive.

Jaclyn Baumgarten

CEO of Boatsetter

Jaclyn Baumgarten is the cofounder and CEO of Boatsetter, a boat rental marketplace with over five thousand boats in six hundred locations. A graduate of Stanford Business School and an IBM, PwC and Westfield corporation Alumna, her grit and vision has allowed her Fort Lauderdale-based company to pioneer the the online marketplace that makes large-scale, peer-to-peer boat rental possible. Under Jaclyn's stewardship, Boatsetter has grown into the market leader in its sector.

What was your entrepreneurial path?

I'm not your stereotypical twenty-something entrepreneur that started straight out of school, pursuing an idea. For me, making sure that I had a very solid and strong foundation in business, building teams and leading organizations was core. I started as a strategy consultant for Fortune 500 companies in New York, then I went to Stanford for my MBA.
My dream was to literally build things, so after Stanford I got a job at Westfield Corporation, one of the largest shopping center developers in the country. They had this competition between Harvard and Stanford each year to pick one person to be put into an executive rotational training program, and I was very fortunate to be selected. After the training program, I ran the largest development project in the city of LA. It was a two-million-square-foot mixed-use project. I oversaw entitlements, feasibility, design, pre-construction, you name it. That was an exceptional opportunity for growth, because I was one of a small handful of Westfield developers at the time under the age of forty-five and probably one of the only females running a development of that magnitude in the entire city of LA.

In 2009 when the market tanked, I went to work with the gentleman who ran all of marketing and operations for the US centers, and he turned to me and said, "Jackie, find a way to make more money out of our existing centers." This was a great opportunity for me to be entrepreneurial under the aegis of a larger corporation. I wrote the business plan and launched a subsidiary called Westfield Media Group in the US. I did that for a little over a year, and by year three they were generating sixty million in incremental revenue for the company.

Those projects really allowed me to learn a tremendous amount about launching and running nascent operations. They gave me confidence and allowed me to build the expertise, the skill set, the emotional intelligence to be able to lead teams, and to really know what it means to be an operator. After that, I was confident that I had the skills I was going to need to bring something new to market and build it on my own.

How did the idea for the company come about?
The question was, "Okay, I'm ready, but what do I want to build?" So I thought about my happiest memories as a kid, and they were being out on the water in the summers with my brothers and my dad. It was one of the few times that my dad, who's also a workaholic, was completely present and aware, and some of our happiest memories were built that way.
I wanted to make that kind of experience available to everyone. At the time, I knew that the biggest challenge of being able to monetize a very expensive and underutilized asset like a boat was the fact that your recreational insurance policy on a boat excludes coverage if you rent or charter. You cannot rent it out, just like you can't just go rent out your own private car. Before a marketplace like Boatsetter could exist, I had to solve the fundamental problem with insurance. So I spent eight months hitting the global insurance markets to convince them to create a policy. I really viewed them – the insurers – as investors and strategic partners in what we were trying to build. It took eight months, and I was finally successful in getting one of the leading maritime underwriters out of the UK to provide the insurance product I had envisioned.

What early struggles did you have, and how did you overcome them while starting out?
First, it was how to solve the insurance problem. Then it was, okay, how do we build a marketplace when I don't have the cash? I had a bit of survival money saved up from my past years working. I put my condo on the market and moved everything I had into storage. I used that as my seed capital and didn't take a salary for two years. I believe that to be a successful entrepreneur, you have to be fully committed! The next challenge after creating the insurance was fundraising, which, as every startup CEO knows, is a Sisyphean task – as soon as one round is closed, you're starting to raise your next round. The next major challenge was getting the equilibrium between supply and demand in place. Now it's scaling and getting the right team in. The challenges continue, you know what I mean? They just change depending on the lifecycle of the company. The challenges never go away; overcoming challenges is essentially what building and running a company is.

"*I don't believe necessarily that you make the right decision; you make the decision right.*"

What was your biggest mistake?

Here's the philosophy I follow: I don't believe necessarily that you make the right decision; you make the decision right. There are many paths to getting something done, so I don't feel as though there were any major mistakes in the path we took. You simply take the best decision and action you can in a given moment, then you assess the good and bad that came out of that decision, then you take another decision and action to correct and continue, and so on and so on... With the benefit of hindsight, there are certainly lessons I've gained and things I'd do differently, but I wouldn't call anything a mistake at this point; they are simply things I'll be able to do better the next time they come up.

What was your best decision?

So here's how I would flip that: I would think about, what is my best quality that has helped me survive and thrive. Because it's not just about one decision; it's about a character trait that is applied to every decision. And that is unwavering grit and tenacity. That has allowed me to survive and thrive in situations where most people would have folded and decided to step out. For example, early on there was my company and another competitor in the marketplace, and we were competing head to head for major deals and partnerships. I'd been making great progress with one of the largest manufacturers in the country and was meeting with their senior management, who told me we had a deal we were about to close. Then, out of leftfield, I get notified that they're going to be closing a deal with my competitor because of a relationship someone on their board had. That was crushing, because it was a strategic partner that was going to provide the critical funding I needed to survive early on, and it would have given us access to supply in a cost-effective way. When I got the call and realized that this deal was taking place with my competitor, it was devastating. I pulled several of my advisors together and said, "What do I do?" One of them, the one I should have fired earlier, said, "It's time to fold up shop."

I was absolutely unwilling to accept that, and so I fought and scraped and scrapped my way to continue to build over the years. And the beauty is that last summer, I acquired that competitor, and I now have the relationship with that manufacturer.

What do you wish you'd known before you started, and what would you have done differently?

There are two things that come to mind: one is related to external fundraising and the other is related to building out a team. In terms of external fundraising, when you're dealing with seed and angel investors, you have to be fiercely protective of your time and a be a master in reading what kind of no's are said, even when the word "no" isn't spoken. There are a lot of people who are just passing their time, being curious, setting up lunches, meetings, coffees, wanting to talk to entrepreneurs. They have no real intention of funding, and it's very easy to waste a ton of time. Your most valuable asset as a founder is your time. You have to learn to be fiercely protective of it. And because early on you build your confidence as you go, I made a mistake that I absolutely would not make today. That mistake is that I didn't fire people fast enough. There are two major categories when you think about the matrix of evaluating somebody as a hire: there's their skill set, and then there's their cultural/personality fit. It's essential that both are there. Early on, I felt this sort of sense of desperation of having someone in the chair who had the skill set, and I provided far too much leniency on the fact that culturally, this person wasn't the right fit. Over time, a bad cultural/personality fit can breed toxicity, and it taints the environment that you need to excel as a team. You have to make the hard decisions early on to cut someone if both the skillset and the fit with the culture are not there.

What professional advice would you give people in the early stages of starting out?

I would strongly encourage that individual to do some serious soul-searching and be truly honest with themselves. They should ask, "Do you have what it takes to take on this journey?" Because if they're thinking about doing it part time while maintaining their other full-time job, then they don't have what it takes. If they're not willing to put everything at risk, then they don't have what it takes. If they're not willing to put their reputation, their relationships, their credibility on the line, and put their own money in first, then they don't have what it takes. Be prepared for suffering.

And what do you like about working in Miami?

I was in San Francisco when I founded the company, and I moved out here simply because Fort Lauderdale is the boating capital of the world. Since I've been here, I've discovered that there are a lot of ancillary benefits to being in South Florida. This is a burgeoning market, so there's a lot of attention and energy and excitement around this entrepreneurial community. You can get great talent here and keep talent here that you can't get in Silicon Valley because of the competition and the skyrocketing cost of talent there.

[About] Boatsetter.com makes boat rental accessible to all consumers regardless of their boating experience. By bringing the sharing economy to the boating industry, they help boat owners capitalize on an investment that sits idle for 95 percent of the time.

[Links] **Web:** boatsetter.com **Facebook:** Boatsetter **Twitter:** @boatsetter **Instagram** Boatsetter

What are your top work essentials?
I always have a notebook and am constantly
reiterating my list for prioritization.

At what age did you found your company?
I think thirty-four.

What's your most-used app?
Gmail.

**What's the most valuable piece of advice
you've been given?**
Don't worry about making the right decision.
Focus on making the decision right. Everything
comes down to execution.

What's your greatest skill?
My ability to couple emotional intelligence with an
analytical mind and apply both to managing my team
and decision-making simultaneously.

Rebekah Monson

Cofounder and COO of WhereBy.Us

Small-town Alabama native Rebekah Monson is one of the three founders of WhereBy.Us and serves as COO. The media startup was created in 2015, and in the spring of 2018 it closed on a $1.5 million investment round at the same time that it secured an undisclosed amount from angel investor Jason Calcanis. Rebekah is the tech and organizational wizard at the heart of the company's efforts to remake the local media landscape.

What was your entrepreneurial path?

It was a rather meandering path. I started my career in journalism. I'd gone to college for that and then worked as a copyeditor, then as a news designer, an art director, a web editor, and a reporter – so I did a ton of different jobs in journalism, and that's kind of my main background. I was looking for a change, and I'd been building websites since I was in high school, like back in the GeoCities days. I decided I wanted to take a run at really getting serious about that, so I got a job at UM [University of Miami] and started grad school in their Interactive Media MFA program. While in school, I ended up cofounding these two organizations here in Miami: a journalism/tech meetup called Hacks/Hackers Miami, and a civic tech meetup that is still making awesome stuff without me, called Code for Miami. We did a lot of work around open data and civic stuff, and along the way I started working with my cofounders Christopher Sopher and Bruce Pinchbeck on WhereBy.Us.

Is that how the idea for the company came about?

Chris started it out as a meetup to do design-thinking around city challenges. We were doing these little ideation exercises around how to get more people to use transit, how to make commuting more delightful, and that was really fun. In the process of doing that, it was sort of like, "Man, there's an opportunity here to serve all these smart young people who want to do more in Miami." So we did a big research project about that and talked to a bunch of people. We were looking at millennials and their information habits, and asking how they learning about the city, and how they got engaged in the city. We thought there was an opportunity to fill this new community and information need, and so we started with the New Tropic in 2015 as a daily email newsletter. We also did a lot of events to bring those people together more and learn about them and what they want to do here in the city.

What early struggles did you have, and how did you overcome them while starting out?

The key with a startup is that you're really trying to scale at an inhuman, almost irrational pace, so you're trying to grow super-duper fast. I think the big challenges we've faced have largely extended around that. Part of being in a startup is being forced to grow before you're ready or before you know how, and that's a great thing, but it's also hard and complicated, and it means you have to adapt to different kinds of work habits and different workflow priorities within the organization.

There's the old axiom about putting in your ten thousand hours; well, the only thing I think we got to spend ten thousand hours on initially was putting out the newsletter, which I think we're pretty excellent at now, but we were also learning so much about making choices and decisions with data and learning how to iterate on our work. I would say that ability to learn and iterate is the super-power we're developing as a company and as a team, but it's also painful to develop, because most of us aren't used to working at that pace and with that amount of focus and intention.

What was your biggest mistake?

Too much tortured decision-making sometimes. I think we try to be really conscientious about who we serve and what our mission is, and we try to apply that to problem-solving. Sometimes that means we should be moving on stuff faster than we realize. I'll tell you one example. Initially when we started the company, Chris and Bruce, like many people in their twenties, had this inclination that we should have a physical space that would basically be like a bar/clubhouse in our office, where we could host events and do parties and hang out with users and those kinds of things. We did that for about a year because we loved the idea of it. We had a space in Little River, and we did a bunch of events there; but we bit off more than we could chew, because we were trying to manage the space as an event venue, plus we were learning all this media and

"If you're good, I suspect you're making mistakes all the time."

tech stuff. When we looked at the numbers and had a heart-to-heart about where the company should go, we knew we'd probably tried to work on events in this way for too long because we were so interested in the idea. We didn't know how all the things we were making fit together yet. We probably didn't need to run our own event venue; we could have just used all the other great venues in town. But we had to try and fail at it to learn and to realize how to set goals smarter and make decisions in a more focused way.

What was your best decision?

I think our team has been our best decision. We have an amazing team of people. We hired really smart, really dedicated, incredibly mission-driven human beings who are willing to do really hard work, take a bunch of smart, calculated risks, try new things, and push themselves really hard. To me, without those people our business would be nothing, and I'm really proud of our team and the people.

What do you wish you'd known before you started, and what would you have done differently?

I think I wasn't prepared for how much business knowledge is required, and that has been a personal journey. One thing that I definitely wasn't expecting was how many business books and stuff like that I'd read. I've read more of those in the past three years of my life than I ever did in the previous thirty-whatever. I feel like you're constantly learning, and that's great. I love that part of the job, but I don't think I realized or was prepared for this sort of singular existence that you need to make a company great, and quickly. If you're really serious about growing, scaling and building a business, it has to become this huge dominant force in your life, and you can't let yourself get thrown off track by all the other million interesting things there are to do. I mean, hell, part of the reason you go into journalism is because you get to explore new stuff all the time, right? But working on the same project when that's kind of your mindset, and learning to find as much joy in working on all the minute problems you can think of within this focused scope of your business, that's a cool thing to do.

What professional advice would you give people in the early stages of starting out?
The first one is to focus: find ways to slim down your schedule, and focus on the things that are important here. I think all those time-management skills … anything you can do to clean up those habits is going to benefit you in a huge way. I think you have to prioritize learning all the things you don't know. Start reading outside your comfort zone. Learning about business fundamentals was a huge thing for me. Like, understanding basic finance concepts, management, simple accounting and things like that. I think those are things you need to get under your belt fast.

The other thing is: ask for help. I don't know what I would have done without help. But I think a lot of people are afraid to ask for help, particularly in the early stages where you have a lot to prove. I don't know how you get through without learning from others, because there are too many lessons. There's so much that you're learning, and you need the shortcut of having really trusted, smart, brilliant people to help you along the way.

And what do you like about working in Miami?
I love Miami. I love everything about Miami. Miami is a city that you're able to shape with whatever your vision is and whatever muscle you're willing to put in. Miami helps to make that happen. I love that. I think that if we'd tried to start in any other city, we'd have a whole lot of different kinds of roadblocks that just are not a challenge here. People are welcoming to new ideas. There's room to experiment. People are excited to help you along the way, if they see that you're serious about the work and that you're putting in as much energy and thought and labor as you can. There are tons of people here who are ready to feed it to you.
I love that about this community.

[About]   WhereBy.Us helps citizens to better connect with their city. With an innovative business model that engages in three verticals (local news delivered via email, software publishing and branded content). Its mission is to "help curious locals make the most of their cities," and they are currently doing just that in four urban areas on two coasts. The company is aggressively expanding to fill the vacuum left behind after a decade of declining journalism ad revenues.

[Links]   Web: whereby.us Facebook: wherebyus Twitter: @WhereByus Instagram @wherebyus

What are your top work essentials?
Laptop. I work all over the place all over the world.

At what age did you found your company?
Thirty-three.

What's your most-used app?
Slack and Zoom, and spreadsheets. I spend a lot of time
in spreadsheets.

**What's the most valuable piece of advice
you've been given?**
"There's always something to learn."

What's your greatest skill?
My greatest skill is learning. You have to know how
to learn, and you have to learn all the time.

Ryan Cohen

Founder and Former CEO / Chewy

At thirty-two years old, when he sold his online pet store Chewy to PetSmart for over $3 billion, Ryan Cohen found himself in rare territory for an entrepreneur: at the very top. Ryan's sale of Chewy was the largest-ever ecommerce acquisition. It was at once a resounding validation of his mission to build the greatest pet retailer, and of his effort – six years of almost nonstop work, more than one hundred rejections from venture capitalists and billions of dollars in sales.

Tell me a little bit about where you come from. Have you always felt like an entrepreneur at heart?
I was born in Canada and grew up in a middle-class neighborhood. My father was a business owner and my mother was a teacher. I learned the value of hard work and of being dedicated at a young age. I saw the sacrifices they made for us and for their work, and that sowed the seeds and gave me the skills needed to be an entrepreneur. I think entrepreneurship, in a lot of ways, requires being selfless. It's doing a lot of work that isn't fun. It was also clear early on in my childhood that I wanted to be my own boss. According to my parents, at age five or six when I'd get into arguments with my older brother and he would say, "I'm the big boss; you're the little boss," I'd get very upset. I'd always yell back at him, "I'm the big boss!"

What's the origin story behind Chewy?
We were actually about to get into a totally different line of business: selling jewelry online. We'd built the website and bought hundreds of thousands of dollars of jewelry. We weren't passionate about the category, but we thought it was underpenetrated online. Literally right before we launched, maybe a week or two, I was shopping at a pet store. I love my dog – and suddenly it just hit me that this was a much bigger opportunity, and we were much more passionate about this space. The pet category at the time was also underpenetrated online,

and there was no company that was dedicated to providing a really good online experience. The vision was to replicate the personal experience at the neighborhood pet store, but do it online and at scale.

How did you go from saying, "Oh, this is a good idea," to actually growing and scaling the business?

There was no business plan or anything like that. We had the idea, we sold the jewelry for pennies on the dollar, we started contacting local distributors to procure product and we just basically learned as we went. From the time we had the idea until when we were actually online was probably about three to four months, and during that time it was just 24/7.

Was there ever a moment in those first months when you were like, "You know what, this is not worth it. I'm just going to keep going to the pet store because that works fine"?

I'm too determined in general to quit when I want to do something. The thought never crossed my mind. I decided early on I saw an opportunity to turn Chewy into a household name and build a large business. I think you'd probably have had to kill me and the team to stop us. Quitting wasn't an option.

Along this path, what were some of the key milestones?

The milestones were revenue growth because scale was critical to our success. We knew that if we wanted to build a durable business market leadership was important. So some of the key milestones were getting $10 million in sales, $100 million in sales, $1 billion. There were other kinds of milestones too, like team count, launching fulfillment centers, and so on.

Looking back, is there anything you would have done differently?

The biggest challenge was adapting to the growth. If you think about retailers, both online and physical, that have scaled from zero to one billion in sales in their first five years, you could count them on one hand. As an example, I remember when we signed the lease on our first distribution center, it was a 400,000 ft² building in Pennsylvania, and I was like, "Wow, this is huge." It was only a few months after that we expanded the building to 800,000 ft². So that became the new standard size for Chewy's future fulfillment centers. As time went on, we learned to adapt and get ahead of it, but that kind of growth curve was unprecedented. Chewy was always making history.

"Having good instincts is critical. Moving forward and pivoting is much safer than not moving forward at all."

At the peak, when you experienced that hypergrowth, what was a day in the life like for you?

In the beginning, it's like drinking from a firehose. I'm making all the key decisions myself. Then, as we scaled and built the leadership team, I started delegating decisions and replacing my daily work load. By delegating decisions, it freed up my time and allowed me to focus on strategy and bigger picture stuff. You go from being front and center of all of the decisions to taking a step back by building a strong leadership team. And in order for those leaders to scale, they have to replicate that behavior too. It's really important as a startup to go through that process. The early days gave me the ability to learn everything about the business: I was answering customer calls and live chats, negotiating with vendors, signing distribution center leases, etc. As you delegate those decisions to your leaders, you transfer the tribal knowledge as well. Understanding the details but being able to delegate decisions is essential to being a good leader.

What advice do you have for early-stage entrepreneurs?

You should be ready to dedicate yourself to your mission. Nobody changes the world and builds a disruptive business without working their butt off. A lot of people fantasize about being an entrepreneur and think it's just about coming up with a novel idea. It's actually the opposite. You don't need the best idea to be successful. What you do need is to be capable of executing. When you're in startup mode, executing means making decisions quickly and taking calculated risks. There's lots of decisions that need to be made on a daily basis, and sometimes you need to be comfortable making them without having complete data. Having good instincts is critical. Moving forward and pivoting is much safer than not moving forward at all.

I'd say the other thing is that you're always going against the tide. In life, it's easy to take the path of least resistance, but being an entrepreneur and building something from scratch requires going against the grain and being OK with being misunderstood. As you go along the journey of building your business, there are a ton of distractions, lots of shiny objects, and everyone around you has their opinion. You better be good at blocking that out, because you've got finite time and capital and must dedicate your resources accordingly. With respect to finances and fundraising in general, my advice is to know your numbers inside and out. Because if you don't, who does? And knowing your numbers and permeating that rigor and discipline into the culture early on is critical. You should know where you're spending every dollar. And if you don't, then good luck raising capital and building a durable business.

What is your entrepreneurship "superpower"?

I'm comfortable taking risks and being contrarian when I believe in something. If you think about the pet category when we started, nobody was interested – especially the investors. I spoke to over a hundred of them, and they all turned me down. When you tell people that your plan is to be a vertically integrated ecommerce company in a commodity category like the pet space, they kind of look at you funny. There was pets.com that failed during the dot com era and Amazon already in the category, so it wasn't a novel idea. But I saw an opportunity and thought we could do it better. From day one we decided we were going to be a customer-obsessed company, and a lot of the decisions we made early on were more intuitive. How do you measure the ROI of sending out customers handwritten holiday cards and pet portraits? We thought it would engage customers, but we didn't know their lifetime value. We just knew it was an emotional category and felt it was the right thing to do.

What comes next for you now that you've stepped down as CEO?

I'm still figuring it out. I'm doing a lot of reflecting and letting everything sink in. The past eight years have flown by. I'm spending more time with my family and learning how to adapt to a slower pace. But I'm definitely an adrenaline junkie. I love fast-growing businesses, and I love talking to entrepreneurs who think big and are building disruptive models. So if you're in the business of delighting your customers and have the opportunity to scale into something much larger, then we should talk!

What do you like most about working in the Miami area?

First, Chewy has the best customer service and that team was grown to over one thousand folks in Florida, so there's an amazing workforce and talent here. Second, being that South Florida is a less popular startup hub than places like Silicon Valley or New York, it's a lot easier to build something and stand out. That helps with hiring and retention as well. And Florida is very business-friendly and offers a great quality of life that's appealing to candidates from across the country.

[About]   Chewy isn't just an online pet store. The company helps pet owners personalize their online shopping experience, interact with qualified salespeople and learn about how to best serve their pets' needs.

[Links]   Web: chewy.com Facebook: Chewy Twitter: @chewy Instagram. chewy

What are your top work essentials?
A constant supply of chocolate. Some people drink
coffee. I eat chocolate.

At what age did you found your company?
Twenty-six.

What's your most-used app?
Apple Music.

**What's the most valuable piece of advice
you've been given?**
Don't follow the crowd.

What's your greatest skill?
Staying focused.

ools

- **Be a girl. We don't have a preferred type.**
  We tweak the curriculum to match where you're coming from, either the artsy side or the logical side.

- **Be open to learning.**
  If you're coming from the creative side, we'll focus on that. If you're more on the math side, we'll introduce you to programming and then show you the art. We pick up on what the student is particularly interested in and go from there.

- **Don't be scared of the math.**
  We tend to get a lot of girls who see themselves as more creative and wouldn't naturally have signed up for a programming class.

- **Stay involved.**
  As girls age out of CodeHER clubs, they can go back and volunteer for that club.
  For example, one of our past students is now going to be the lead instructor at our FIU-based CodeHER club starting up this fall.

Code/Art

[Elevator Pitch]

"We got girls excited about computer science by showing them the creative side of coding through an art-infused curriculum. We're building an on-ramp to computer science for elementary and middle school girls."

[Name]

[Enrollment]

Last year, we had fifty-five students in three weekly coding clubs. This year, we're expanding to six clubs and expect to have about 120 girls in weekly clubs.

[Description]

The percentage of women graduating with a bachelor's degree in computer science has dropped from 37 percent in 1984 to 18 percent today. The reasons are numerous: boys being introduced to computing at an earlier age than girls; stereotypes about coders being mostly male; and the pernicious idea that computer science needs to be an impassionate, uncreative endeavor. Code/Art wants to change this. Founded in 2016, it has inspired more than 1,200 girls in grades three to twelve to get involved in coding through art.

The idea is to meet girls where they are and show them that coding can be creative and catered to their interests. Code/Art offers after-school CodeHER clubs and weekend workshops with the Girl Scouts of Tropical Florida and other community partners, and runs a monthly school-wide program at a local all-girls school. "If girls wait until high school to start coding, they're less likely to stick with it. By then, the guys know all the lingo. They seem so ahead of the game, and it can be discouraging," says Amy Austin Renshaw, cofounder and executive director at Code/Art. "We want to level the playing field to give girls access, so that when they do meet up in that first computer science class in high school, they aren't already behind."

The year-long programs culminate each spring in Code/Art Miami, an event that brings together girls from across South Florida to showcase the artwork they created using code. Code/Art also runs school-day programs, hosts weekend workshops in partnership with other nonprofits and corporations, and runs "Hour of Code" workshops during Computer Science Education Week. Thanks to a $25,000 grant from United Way's Inspire305 initiative, Code/Art hopes to double its programming offerings next year. "There's a ladder up," Amy says. "Our mission is to get girls to code all the way through college, to graduate, and to go into a tech job."

[Apply to] **code-art.com**

[Links] Web: **code-art.com** Facebook: **codeartmiami** Twitter: **@CodeArtMiami**

- **Have an innovative solution to a problem.**
  You're looking for the 10X improvement to the current solution to a problem and a large group of customers that need a solution.

- **Be open to receiving coaching.**
  Entrepreneurship is an iterative process, and we're looking for individuals and teams that instinctively know this fact and willingly process all forms of input to make better decisions.

- **Have the ability and desire to do the research.**
  The discovery and understanding of the natural and social sciences informs and enriches our lives. We want those who appreciate this richness.

- **Have a salesperson's mentality.**
  Creating an MVP and beginning to get traction in the marketplace through sales is a challenge that separates unsuccessful and successful entrepreneurs.

[Name]

Florida International University

[Elevator Pitch]

"We're a university-wide initiative to foster innovation and entrepreneurship to pursue opportunities in the Fourth Industrial Revolution, including the developing breakthrough technologies, pursuing enterprises that close social or environmental gaps and creating companies that create meaningful jobs."

[Enrollment]

54,000

[Description]

Located in what was once an abandoned airfield, Florida International University has grown into one of the country's biggest universities – home to more than fifty thousand students – and it is the only public research institute in the state of Florida. The university ranks highly in a number of fields, including international business, hospitality, and its online criminal justice program. Since 2016, its flagship entrepreneurship program, StartUP FIU, has supported researchers, inventors, innovators and entrepreneurs to conceive, launch and scale solutions to social and market problems. "It is such an exciting time to be an innovator," says Emily Gresham, assistant vice president of research at FIU and cofounder of StartUP FIU. "New technologies have lowered many of the barriers to start your own company, but in order to really be able to pursue these opportunities, you need to be equipped with the knowledge and tools."

StartUP FIU offers an application-only prototyping studio, business accelerator and food incubator programs. The Proof of Concept Studio is a six-week course for early-stage researchers, inventors and entrepreneurs to prototype their ideas and take the first steps towards commercialization. The Empower Accelerator is a fourteen-week program designed to help entrepreneurs with early-stage companies become venture-ready. StartUP FIU Food offers commercial kitchen space and technical assistance to help food entrepreneurs scale their operations. "We're interested in working with anyone who wants to have an impact on this fast changing world," Emily says. "We want to support innovation that is human-centric and improves our lives."

One of StartUP FIU's unique aspects is that it's available not just to students, faculty and alumni but to anyone in the greater Miami area. "FIU takes its role as a public research university seriously," Emily says. "We feel a responsibility to find better ways to address issues like poverty, income inequality and environmental sustainability. We're an anchor in the community and want to harness Miami's energy in innovation and entrepreneurship to initiate the change we want to see."

[Apply to]

Empower Accelerator: Email startupempwr@fiu.edu

[Links]

Web: **startup.fiu.edu** Facebook: **startupfiu** Twitter: **@startupfiu** Instagram: **@startupfiu**

- **Have a passion for tech.**
  We want people who care about the work
  and are not just in it for the money.

- **Be committed to hard work.**
  This will be the most intense learning experience
  of your life, so you must be prepared to dedicate
  yourself.

- **Submit a written application form.**
  The written application includes a series of questions
  that seek to better understand why you want
  to attend Ironhack.

- **Come in for an interview.**
  Our admission representative will meet with
  you to determine if you're a good fit.

- **Take a technical assessment.**
  Prospective students must complete a thirty-minute
  programming challenge that requires eight hours
  of preparation. The assessment helps us determine
  which students will be committed to the process.

[Name]

Ironhack

[Elevator Pitch]

"We're a global tech school that trains adults in the most relevant twenty-first-century digital skills, with operations in Miami, Europe and Latin America."

[Enrollment]

43 students enrolled. 364 total graduates.

[Description]

Ironhack is an international technology school that places an emphasis on helping students acquire digital skills and employment in tech. Cofounders Ariel Quiñones and Gonzalo Manrique met in the MBA program at the Wharton School of Business in 2011. The duo wanted to create a tech-education program for places like Spain and Latin America, where youth unemployment is high and where there's a high demand for IT and coding skills. After successfully launching schools in Madrid and Barcelona, Ironhack opened a Miami campus in 2014. "We saw the buzz and excitement around Miami as a tech hub," says Ariel. "We thought that we could help supply the area with the talent and skills to help that come to fruition."

Ironhack offers full-time and part-time programs in web development, user experience design and data analytics. The full-time program lasts ten weeks while the part-time program lasts six months. Each course is project-based, giving students the opportunity to apply their education to solving real-world problems. "The best way to learn how to program or design is to do it yourself," Ariel says. "We develop your programming and design muscles by simulating real-world work environments."

The final week of each program is dedicated to career services. Employers from fifteen to forty different companies will come to Ironhack and interview students. Ironhack also offers resume building services, job interview preparation and networking and alumni events. Ironhack Miami is located out of Building.co, a coworking space for Miami tech companies. The school features two dedicated classrooms, a communal space and unlimited coffee and beer on tap. Students also have access to Ironhack campuses in Madrid, Barcelona, Amsterdam, Berlin, Paris, Mexico City and Sao Paulo. "Giving access to tech ecosystems in all of our cities is a really nice value add to help students develop their careers in multiple markets," Ariel said.

[Apply to]   ironhack.com/en/courses/web-development-bootcamp/apply

[Links]   Web: **ironhack.com/en** Facebook: **theironhack** Twitter: **@ironhack** Instagram: **ironahackmia**

- **Be driven.**
  Do you demonstrate the motivation to improve your circumstances? Do you want to learn more about tech, and can you demonstrate that through the things you're saying in your application?

- **Show some degree of prior interest in tech.**
  We look for students who have a demonstrated curiosity about tech and the tech industry.

- **Have a knack for problem-solving.**
  We want individuals who have a knack for problem-solving. It doesn't have to be within the context of computer programs. It can include anything from Sudoku puzzles to word games.

- **Don't be afraid to ask questions.**
  The first step to getting involved is knowing the resources that can let you know what's happening. Once you know what's happening, you can pick the things that are in your wheelhouse of interest.

[Name]
LaunchCode

[Elevator Pitch]
"We're building a skilled workforce by creating pathways for driven people seeking careers in technology. We help job-seekers enter the tech field by providing accessible education, training and paid apprenticeship job placement."

[Enrollment]
150 in each course; about 800 total students have gone through Miami's program

[Description]
Stereotypes of a bespectacled coder living in his parents' basement be damned. The face of coding is changing, and as it shifts – becoming younger, more diverse, more female – LaunchCode is leading the charge. Originally founded in St. Louis, LaunchCode has grown into a truly national organization with programs in Kansas City, Tampa Bay, Washington D.C. and Miami. It provides free coding lessons to individuals who have been traditionally left behind and who continue to be underrepresented in the tech world. "LaunchCode makes a good-paying career in technology accessible to people who might not otherwise have that opportunity," says Matt Mawhinney, director of Candidate Engagement at LaunchCode. "All of our classes are free, and we do broad-based outreach through partner organizations that target underrepresented communities."

Founded in 2013, LaunchCode expanded to Miami one year later and has provided free coding lessons to more than eight hundred students in South Florida. Through LaunchCode's flagship program, LC 101, students learn two different coding languages – Python and C# – and complete a capstone project. They also receive employment prep, go through job readiness training, and complete a paid apprenticeship, meaning that when they complete the program, they're ready to jump right into full-time employment.

LaunchCode's student body reflects the diversity of the various communities it serves. In Miami, for example, 80 percent of students are students of color, 32 percent are women and 25 percent were previously unemployed before joining the program. And while students come into the program at different levels of experience, four in five students will leave with a full-time job in tech. "What someone is going to come out with is professional web development skills, and they're also going to have worked on professional development within the context of the tech industry," Matt says. "We're part of making a dent in those stats."

[Apply to]
launchcode.org/lc101

[Links]
Web: **launchcode.org** Facebook: **launchcode.org** Twitter: **@launchcode**

- **Be serious about learning.**
  You should be open to new experiences and ideas, passionate about innovation, entrepreneurship and technology, and curious about how you can apply your knowledge to solve issues both big and small.

- **Be open to a diverse learning experience.**
  We want a diverse learning environment where student from all walks of life and all parts of the world can collaborate with others who have travelled their own unique path.

- **Be committed.**
  The Idea Center offers programs that are mentally rigorous, and we are only looking for students who are willing and able to see it through to completion.

- **Have a vision.**
  We want students who can develop innovative solutions to meet America's most pressing economic and social challenges.

[Name]

Miami Dade College / The Idea Center

[Elevator Pitch]

"We seek to enable all Miami Dade College students to succeed in a disruptive, knowledge-based economy by teaching them world-class innovation, technology and entrepreneurship skills."

[Enrollment]

150,000

[Description]

With the largest undergraduate student enrollment in the country, Miami Dade College caters to a diverse, multilingual student body. It is, in essence, a microcosm of the city of Miami itself. And at The Idea Center, students can take advantage of affordable programs in entrepreneurship and technology that help them to develop twenty-first-century skills. Launched in 2014 with a grant from Knight Foundation, The Idea Center is available to all Miami Dade College students. What makes the Idea Center unique, according to Executive Director Romi Bhatia, is that it offers skills and expertise to an often underserved population. "Two thirds of our students are low income," Romi says. "As an open-access institution, it's our responsibility to be a cog in the entrepreneurial ecosystem and equip our students for success."

The Idea Center provides several different courses in entrepreneurship and technology. In entrepreneurship, there's Startup Challenge, a twelve-week course that guides students as they turn their idea into a working prototype. Students that complete this course can then participate in Create, which helps them to develop a go-to-market strategy over a ten-week period. Students who have an early-stage business can take Scale Up Miami, a free forty-hour program that provides training in operations, marketing and finance.

On the technology side of things, students can take classes in information technology, website development, programming and visual storytelling. The technology programs are open to any member of the Miami community and last anywhere from twelve to twenty weeks. Each course costs $399, although there are discounts for Miami Dade College students. The Idea Center also organizes mentoring programs, speaker events and workshops for entrepreneurs. "We don't want to be just a series of programs," Romi says. "We want to prepare people to solve social and market-based challenges in their communities. To do that, we need to make sure everything we provide is affordable and high quality."

[Apply to]

Entrepreneurship programs: theideacenter.co/lean-startup

Technology programs: theideacenter.co/code

[Links]

Web: **theideacenter.co** Facebook: **ideacenterMDC** Twitter: **@ideacentermdc**

- **Be open to feedback and embrace failure.**
  A big part of being mentored is being receptive
  to feedback and learning from your mistakes.

- **Trust the process.**
  Regardless of what stage your idea maybe, our
  suggestions for next steps will help achieve progress.

- **Be looking to make a change.**
  Essential to creating a company is a diversity of
  backgrounds and ideas that can disrupt a market
  in need of rethinking.

- **Show you're comfortable with the unknown.**
  No path is the same when launching a company,
  but that's was brightens the "how we did it" story.

- **Be ready to enter a community of collaborative
  entrepreneurs.**
  Furthering an idea can be as simple
  as a conversation. In order to feel the impact that
  startups create, the larger number the better.

[Name]

The University of Miami / The Launch Pad

[Elevator Pitch]

"We help students, alumni, faculty and staff launch and grow their business via advisory and mentorship services, events and workshops."

[Enrollment]

17,000

[Description]

With programs at the bachelor's, master's and doctoral level and more than fifteen thousand students, the University of Miami is a top-tier private research institution. Its outstanding reputation is not just recognized in Florida but nationwide, with U.S. News & World Report ranking the school forty-fifth in the country. Founded in 2008, The Launch Pad at the University of Miami is a free, campus-wide resource for students, alumni, faculty and staff interested in or already pursuing entrepreneurship. To date it has helped over 4,900 entrepreneurs launch 480 businesses and create 1,500 new jobs. "Entrepreneurship is a career choice. The Launch Pad allows its clients, regardless of what degree, job or career path they're on, to make the decision to become a game changer," says Brian Breslin, director of The Launch Pad. "We're here to support the CEO's of the future."

The Launch Pad consists of three full-time staff along with several students. Together the team offers their clients an array of free services, including venture consulting, mentorship programs, speaker events and educational workshops. The office meets with any stage venture from ideation to maturity. Consulting topics include things like identifying target markets, product/market fit, venture capital opportunities, revenue models and fundraising structures. The Launch Pad does not offer legal advice or funding but points clients in the direction where it can be found. New in the making is a free two-thousand square-foot coworking space called SkyLab where clients can work on their ideas. The space is designed to encourage creativity and collaboration with open-space work areas as well as a private conference room. Clients of The Launch Pad come from all backgrounds: "Regardless of your degree, background or knowledge of entrepreneurship, our staff is trained to address your needs and help you move your idea along," Brian says. "If you go to University of Miami and you have an idea for a business, we want to talk to you."

[Apply to]

um.thelaunchpad.org/user/register

[Links]

Web: **um.thelaunchpad.org** Facebook: **TheLaunchPad** Twitter: **@TheLaunchPad**

- **Be malleable.**
  We're looking for passion, drive, commitment and a desire to reinvent yourself.

- **Be ready to put in the hours.**
  Is this something you're going to work really hard at? Do you love it enough to put in those extra hours and weekends?

- **Prepare for the coding challenge.**
  As part of our application process for our Full Stack Program, we ask applicants to attempt a coding challenge, because we believe that having a little bit of exposure really helps our students take on this new education and mindset.

- **Be intellectually curious.**
  We also have our applicants take a test where we look at their cognitive ability and their motivation. This helps us understand the makeup of our class, creatives versus analytical students, entrepreneurs versus those looking to start a new career.

[Name]
Wyncode

[Elevator Pitch]
"We're an accelerated learning program for web development, UX/UI and digital skills. We have two full-time courses: one in web development and the other in user experience and user interface (UX/UI), in addition to part-time programs."

[Enrollment]
The programs have a capacity of twenty-five students each and start every five weeks. Over 600 Wyncoders have graduated since launch.

[Description]
Wyncode could have been founded in LA, Austin or any number of developed and emerging tech markets, but cofounders Juha and Johanna Mikkola had a vision – and Miami was the best fit. In four years, Wyncode, a Wynwood-based coding school that focuses on bringing web development and UX/UI skills to a more diverse population, has graduated more than six hundred students, who are now working at 250 premiere companies around the world. The young program is fast becoming one of the best options for neophyte coders and web developers. "We figured if we could build a better functioning program and launch it in an area where there isn't much technology yet, we could have a big impact in the community," Juha says. "That's what drove us here."

Wyncode's offerings include a full-time, ten-week program on full-stack web development; an eight-week UX/UI immersive course; part-time courses in front-end web development and digital marketing; and various training opportunities for corporate partners. The program endeavors to be accessible to people from all walks of life. The average age of students is twenty-nine, and many have worked in non-tech sectors for at least several years. More than half of students are Hispanic, 10 percent are African-American, and about one-quarter are women. The company has invested more than $1.4 million of its own money toward strengthening the talent pipeline for female coders.

For entrepreneurs looking to create their own company in Miami or elsewhere, Wyncode provides high-quality professional training and an unmatched professional network. For example, two Wyncode graduates turned their final project into a thriving startup that now counts seven Wyncoders among its thirty-plus employees. "We're very welcoming of entrepreneurs," Juha says. "To be a developer, you don't need a university degree, and you don't need to be really good at math. We want to change those preconceptions and get a more diverse population – especially in Miami – into web development."

[Apply to]
wyncode.co

[Links]
Web: **wyncode.co** Facebook: **wyncode** Twitter: **@wyncode** Instagram: **wyncode**

stors

- **Find someone we know to introduce you to us rather than sending a cold email.**
  You'll stand out from everyone else and have a better chance of securing a meeting.

- **Clearly define your customer.**
  Speak to what your customer values most and demonstrate how you plan to deliver that value.

- **The goal of your first investor meeting is to secure a second meeting, not a check.**
  Structure your pitch as a conversation. Aim for a focused dialog so you can learn how your potential investors think and can demonstrate how you think.

- **Don't go it alone.**
  Bring your team member who has the expertise to field questions that you can't. Task them with taking notes on how the pitch went, questions asked, clarity of message, etc. Don't bring consultants.

- **Be memorable.**
  Follow up fast and firm. Answer unanswered questions. Highlight key points. Share where you are in your fundraising process and timeframe. Ask for what you need beyond just cash.

[Name]

Krillion Ventures

[Elevator Pitch]

"We invest in entrepreneurs who challenge the status quo and believe there are simpler, smarter and faster ways to do things. As a Miami-first fund, we prioritize the review of and investment in opportunities based in South Florida. However, our investment portfolio includes companies across the US."

[Sector]

Tech companies solving problems in health and wellness, real estate and finance

[Description]

Krillion Ventures, cofounded by Jeffrey Miller and Melissa Krinzman, calls itself a "Miami-first" fund, which means that while it will invest in any company that matches its thesis, it prioritizes companies coming out of South Florida. "Jeff and I were both born in Miami, and we have an affinity toward our city in terms of its current and future success," says Melissa, managing partner at Krillion Ventures. "When I moved back to South Florida from New York, I saw pockets of entrepreneurial activity, but no connectivity amongst entrepreneurs and no visible early-stage capital. Having been part of New York's tech scene, I knew that a city's continued growth and success depended on the ideas and determination of its entrepreneurs as well the financial fuel provided by local investors. Jeff and I shared this belief and joined forces to launch the first early-stage venture fund here in Miami to give priority to Miami-based companies." They chose the name Krillion Ventures, a fusion of the "Kri" in Krinzman, "ll" in Miller and the suffix "-ion" because "all large numbers end in 'ion.'" The unique name matches the unique nature of the fund.

Founded in 2014, Krillion Ventures invests at the seed stage in companies seeking capital to accelerate their growth. To date, it has invested in twenty-four companies. Depending on the opportunity, their check size ranges from six to seven figures, and the fund will make follow-on investments. Ultimately, their goal is to provide a boost to the Miami startup ecosystem – from within. "Building a startup ecosystem takes time and patience, and the failures appear before the successes. I'm encouraged by our community leaders who have a long-term vision," Melissa says. "We're all working together to build and support a Miami that will be recognized for its tech and innovation as well as for fun and sun."

[Apply to]

oneinakrillion@krillionventures.com

[Links]

Web: krillionventures.com

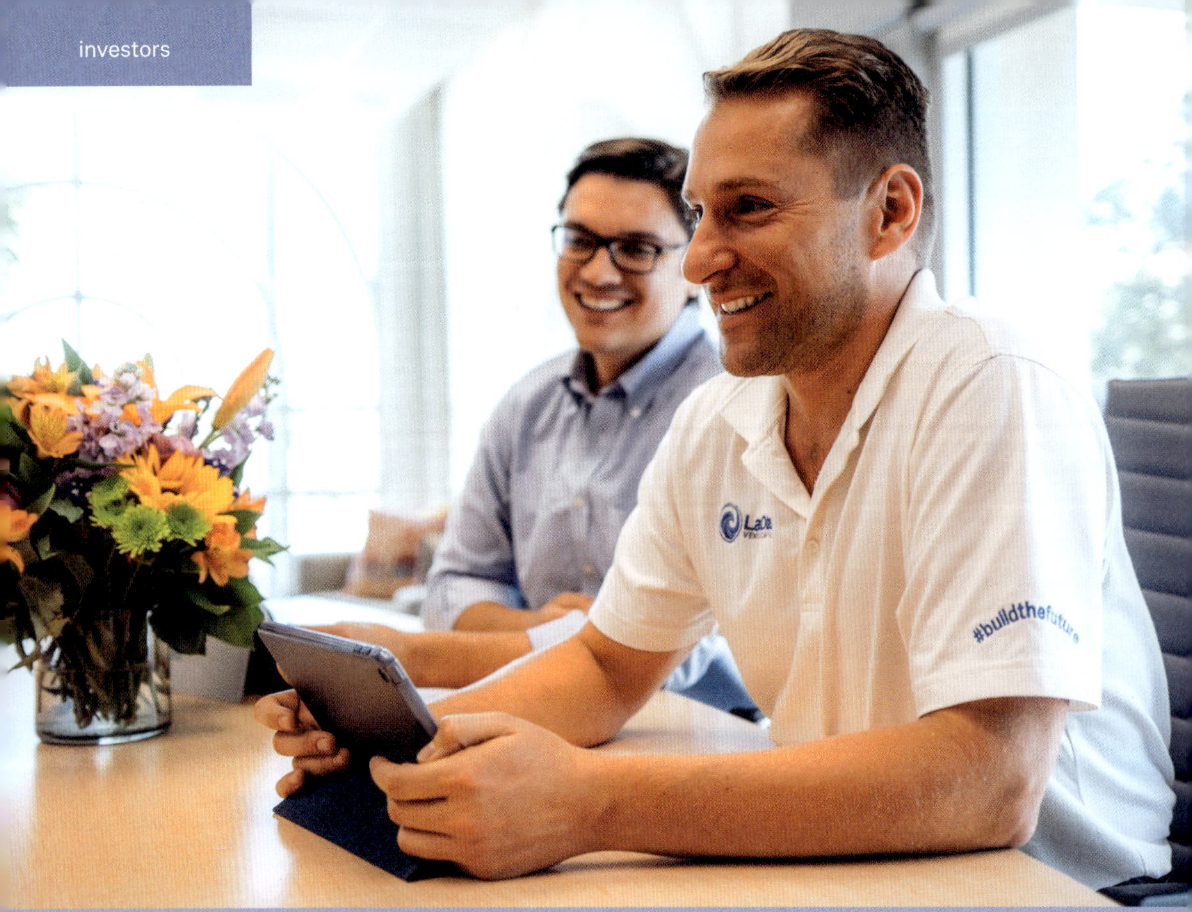

- **Focus on B2B.**
We generally like to invest in B2B companies because that's what we know. We like companies where there's a sales team, a sales process and a sales pipeline.

- **Show early traction.**
It's not just a good team and a good idea, but a good team with the right idea. Ultimately, we don't invest in ideas; we invest in companies that have early traction, so we like to see early customers and a proven product-market fit.

- **Be an insider.**
With most of the businesses we invest in, a random person off the street might not even figure out what the problem is because it's esoteric. Almost all of our founders have prior experience in their field and are doing something that gives them a leg up on someone else who's trying to do it.

- **Have the right connections.**
You should know the industry, and know everybody in the industry.

[Name]

Las Olas Venture Capital

[Elevator Pitch]

"We're an early-stage VC firm that was started by three entrepreneurs. We want to help entrepreneurs build their company from the seed stage until the next round, and then, as a trusted advisor, help them continue through that growth profile."

[Sector]

B2B

[Description]

Las Olas Venture Capital was founded on a simple premise: that the best investors to support early-stage entrepreneurs are successful entrepreneurs themselves. At Las Olas Venture Capital, three of its four founding partners fit the bill. Mark Volchek founded Higher One, a company that manages financial interactions between students and educational institutions electronically, and led it to a successful IPO; Dean Hatton served as CEO for that company; and Esteban Reyes led three different startups to successful exits. "This is really our first endeavor as investors, even though we've all been angel investors for more than ten years," Mark says. "It came out of the realization that in second- and third-tier markets, in smaller cities or cities like Miami that don't have as developed ecosystems, there's a lack of funding between angel investors and existing institutional investors."

Las Olas typically invests in early-stage B2B companies, looking to partner with them and help them through the various steps of funding their startup. The average first check size is $1 million, although investments have ranged from $250,000 to $3.5 million. The firm provides more than just capital investment; it also acts as an operating partner, helping startups recruit talent, interview candidates and get connected to the next round of investors. So far, Las Olas has invested in eight companies in its first fund, including several South Florida-based companies such as Plum, CarePredict and ReloQuest. It plans to raise a second fund in the second half of 2019. These companies, Mark notes, tend to have one thing in common: a focus on "selling, selling, selling." "The most important thing I see too many entrepreneurs wait on or not focus on is selling and getting customers," Mark says. "We try to push entrepreneurs to get ten letters of intent before they even start building a product. Without that, you may think customers want the product, but you may be missing key points in every stage."

[Apply to]

buildthefuture@lasolasvc.com

[Links]

Web: lasolasvc.com Twitter: @lasolasvc LinkedIn: las-olas-venture-capital

- **Be magnetic.**
Magnetic is something that we look for. Can you attract top people? Can you attract amazing clients?

- **Show signs of greatness.**
We want to see things that have made you stand out in anything you've done before.

- **Find your niche.**
We like the little niches that are untapped because we think you can build really interesting companies there with much more interesting market dynamics.

- **Know one another well.**
We tend to like teams or cofounders who have worked together in the past or know each other at a personal level. This is a long, very difficult journey with a lot of missteps, and knowing the person you're riding that journey with is fundamental.

Magnetico Ventures

[Name]

[Elevator Pitch] *"We're a $60 million venture fund focused on being high-conviction seed investors where we lead or colead, working with the founders to put together a tight-knit syndicate."*

[Sector] **Generalist**

[Description] *Young, hungry, scrappy, hardworking:* these are all words typically associated with entrepreneurs, but now Magnetico Ventures, a Miami-based VC upstart, wants these words to be associated with investors as well. Officially founded in July 2018, Magnetico Ventures raised its first venture fund of $60 million. The company is planning a formal launch for late 2018, at which time it will announce its managing partners and initial investments. "We aspire to be the type of human we want to invest in," says Nico Berardi, founder of Magnetico Ventures. "We're in the process of making our first two investments in this fund, but as individuals we've each been in the venture business for five or six years, and we bring a lot from our previous lives as operators."

Magnetico Ventures is especially interested in founders that are building companies in secondary and tertiary ecosystems. By allocating resources to these smaller markets, the VC hopes, in turn, to provide them a bridge to Silicon Valley and New York. In addition to investing in companies, Magnetico Ventures wants to level the playing field between investors and entrepreneurs. The firm will focus on building a genuine relationship with its founders and cutting down on response time (which includes passing quickly on investments that it doesn't care for). It will also track its investments against a set of KPIs that can constantly challenge implicit bias. This means investing in companies led by founders who are diverse in terms of race, gender or background, and in markets that are often overlooked or untapped. "There's this imaginary table that divides entrepreneurs and investors," Nico says. "We want to break away from that. The way we want to be remembered is a VC without ego, without hubris, just three hungry humans trying to partner up with other hungry humans."

[Apply to] hi@magnetico.vc or nico@magnetico.vc

[Links] Web: magnetico.vc Twitter: @magneticovc

- **Be exceptional.**
  We want founders who are ambitious, humble
  and have a thirst for knowledge.

- **Have technology that's unique.**
  Your product should offer consumer or business
  solutions that are innovative.

- **Have a product-market fit.**
  You should be able to show early indicators of market
  validation and revenue generation.

- **Have a product that can cater to very large markets.**
  Ideally, your markets are untapped or underserved
  by existing products.

- **Be a local businesses.**
  All operations must be based in Florida.

- **Have a history of organic growth.**
  You have to put out a product that users
  are delighted by.

[Name]

Miami Angels

[Elevator Pitch]

"We're an angel network with over one hundred investors that invest in early-stage high-growth software ventures with local operations and global reach."

[Sector]

Early-stage investing

[Description]

Miami Angels is comprised of local investors committed to investing in high-impact entrepreneurs. The group formed in 2012 as a way to make it easier for local startups to access capital. Since then, Miami Angels has invested $8 million in twenty-five different Florida-based companies while growing its network to include one hundred accredited angel investors. "Our investors know that investing in tech creates jobs, fosters diversity and makes Miami more sustainable," says Rebecca Danta, managing director at Miami Angels. "Furthermore, we think it's important for members of the South Florida community to be supporting each other."

Miami Angels typically invests in the seed stage of a business. They look for software businesses with traction in the marketplace that need additional capital to fuel growth. The average investment is about $350,000. "We're looking for driven entrepreneurs who are ready to scale," says Rebecca. Some of the businesses Miami Angels has invested in include Blanket, a B2B automated sales rep; Home61, an online real estate brokerage; and NearPod, an app that enables teachers to create and share interactive multimedia presentations with their students.

Miami Angels is made up of professional investors, entrepreneurs and c-suite executives, all of whom are chosen by a member selection committee. All investors must be accredited, bring intellectual capital to the group, and receive an invite in order to join, but Miami Angels also trains investors who are newer to the asset class. Miami Angels is the most active investor group in the city, and has bigger picture plans to establish Miami as a preeminent tech hub. "With easy access to Latin America and Europe, more people are seeing that Miami is a great place to grow and scale a business," Rebecca says. "We want Miami Angels to be their first stop for smart capital."

[Apply to]

miamiangels.vc/apply-for-funding

[Links]

Web: **miamiangels.vc** Twitter: **@MiamiAngelsVC**

- **Fit the profile.**
  I look for companies in ecommerce, ecommerce enablement, social media and social media enablement. Most importantly, I'm investing in talent and a compelling product concept.

- **Have an incredible product sensibility.**
  When I write a check, it's for a founder who probably hasn't found product-market fit yet, so I have to feel that you have an incredible product sensibility to get there, get more funding, scale and grow.

- **Have a big idea.**
  Be able to create a large company in your space. You must have a great product sensibility and be able to demonstrate that, and it must be a big problem you're solving.

- **Don't be a "me too."**
  I don't really like "me-too's." I like originals in their category. And I'm a contrarian. If everyone is chasing an idea or deal, it's probably not for me.

Quixotic Ventures

[Name]

[Elevator Pitch] *"I'm an early-stage investor in mostly consumer internet startups, but also some SAAS. I've invested in a couple dozen companies and will invest up to $250,000, but my initial investment is between $50,000 to $100,000."*

[Sector] **Digital media, social media (and social media enablement) and ecommerce (and ecommerce enablement)**

[Description] Making a successful investment at a very early stage in a startup's lifespan is a fundamentally risky proposition; after all, nine in ten startups will fail. This is why doing so requires being quixotic, or extremely idealistic. Perhaps that idealism is what has made Mark Kingdon, founder of and sole partner at Quixotic Ventures, so good at it. Time and time again, Mark has correctly hedged his bets and managed to find those rare success stories. Early-stage companies he's invested in include the likes of Twitter, Refinery29, TheRealReal and OfferUp. "I'm always looking for compelling startups that are breaking away from the pack," Mark says, "and I go after the things that I like."

While Quixotic Ventures was formally founded just four years ago, Mark has been investing for more than a dozen years. Before that, he served as CEO of three companies. This wealth of experience and deep knowledge of the fields he invests in (digital media, social media and ecommerce) has meant that pretty much from the day he began investing he found significant success. Since its founding, Quixotic Ventures companies have created $27 billion in revenue, generating an eleven times return on investment. Three have been unicorns and six have achieved valuations of more than $100 million. Some of its portfolio companies have indeed fallen short, but the majority go on to raise another round of investment.

The future may be even brighter. "This is one of the most exciting times I've seen to start a company because so many of the technical challenges of the past have been solved, which allows people to take an idea to product really quickly," Mark says. "That's exciting for entrepreneurs, because they can see whether or not the market is responding positively to their product. Development times are shorter, the capital to start a startup is lower, and I think the opportunities are tremendous."

[Apply to] mark@quixotic-ventures.com

[Links] Web: **quixotic.ventures** Twitter: @Markis

- **Have a transformative impact.**
  We look for companies that can scale globally
  and create transformative changes for society.

- **Be in B2C sectors.**
  We're geographically agnostic and generally invest in
  sector-focused B2C companies in consumer products
  and services, fintech and healthcare technology. With
  that in mind, we are open to other types of companies
  and have invested in B2B businesses in the past.

- **Ensure product-market fit.**
  We look for companies that have proven there
  is product-market fit – and not necessarily through
  sales. We've invested in companies that are
  pre-revenue, as long as they have proven
  the usability and acceptability of the product.

- **Demonstrate leadership.**
  We want to see founders and management teams
  who have proven their ability to carry out their visions
  to the fullest extent in their past work.

Secocha Ventures

[Name]

[Elevator Pitch]

"We're a venture capital management firm with a twist. We invest capital from a discretionary fund into companies first, and then lead a syndication effort for a curated network of limited partners on a deal-by-deal basis."

[Sector]

Consumer products and services, fintech, healthcare technology

[Description]

It started off organically. "Friends and family said, 'We like what you're doing; can we piggyback?'" says Sanket Parekh, now managing partner at Secocha Ventures. "Friends of friends, and then friends of those people, started reaching out, and that pivoted into this model." Five years later, Secocha Ventures isn't quite an angel group but it's not a traditional venture capital fund either. Instead, it borrows from both investment playbooks. The result is an investment management firm with a core discretionary fund acting as an anchor, which is then supplemented by a curated group of limited partners (LPs) investing through special purpose vehicles (SPVs) on a deal-by-deal basis, managed by Secocha Ventures. "We have a set of LPs who are not angels," Sanket says." They don't have the time to conduct their own due diligence but like to be involved to a certain level in deciding where their money is invested, and they're willing to write much larger checks than angels. We give them the opportunity to be involved in the decision."

Geographically agnostic, Secocha Ventures has invested in both local and international companies that tend to be B2C-focused, including CarePredict and Home61 (Florida), The Financial Gym and Industrial Organic (New York), Le15 Patisserie (India), and Ossio (Israel). The firm's typical first check is $100,000, but follow-on investments have gone as high as $5 million. The firm is always looking to break into new industries and developing markets, and frequently brings in industry experts for deal review. The Secocha team also manages Pidilite Ventures, the corporate VC arm of Pidilite Industries Ltd, an $8 billion publicly-listed multinational corporation. "What we've recognized is that it's not necessary for us to be in a core VC ecosystem as long as we're able to invest in building networks in those ecosystems," Sanket says. "We have deep relationships with co-investors in Mumbai, New York, the Bay Area, and now we are establishing a similar network in Tel Aviv."

[Apply to]

apply@secocha.com

[Links]

Web: **secocha.com** LinkedIn: **secocha-investments**

- **Be mission-driven.**
  The only rule we will not break is that your
  company's mission fits squarely within ours.

- **Be purposeful and profitable.**
  We believe that, more often than not, the profit
  motive is a strong incentive in the long run to build
  sustainable and valuable businesses. The company
  must address humanity's biggest problems in a
  profitable way, which will enable top-tier financial
  returns on our investment.

- **Find the perfect team.**
  The founding team is the number-one key to a
  successful outcome. We look for innovative founders
  that are at the top of their field and building their
  business with passion as well as pragmatism.

- **Question everything.**
  Our founders tend to be people who look around
  corners, question the things we all take for granted
  and understand that as technology evolves, the
  underlying assumptions might change and reveal
  new ways to solve big problems.

Starlight Ventures

[Name]

Starlight Ventures

[Elevator Pitch] *"We're a new early-stage fund focused on backing entrepreneurs who are addressing humanity's biggest challenges and opportunities."*

[Sector] **Multiple**

[Description] Located just a couple hundred miles south of the Kennedy Space Center, the primary launching point for the majority of NASA's manned and unmanned space vessels, Starlight Ventures is sending off its own moonshots from the sandy beaches of Miami. These ventures, aimed at solving some of humanity's greatest challenges – such as feeding the planet sustainably, increasing healthy lifespans, exploring space and understanding the potential of brain-computer interfaces – constitute calculated investments in the future of humanity. "The next big wave in technology is transformative companies that will make money and simultaneously make the world a better place," says Patricia Wexler, cofounder and managing director at Starlight Ventures.

Starlight Ventures is all about investing in scientists and entrepreneurs who propose solutions to some of the biggest questions, not just on our planet but in our galaxy. For example, Modern Meadow is one of the first startups to develop animal products from cultured cells, while Finless Foods is bio-fabricating clean fish meat to reduce commercial fishing, fish farming and the toxic effects of ocean-pollution in our diets. Skyloom Global is developing laser technology to debottleneck satellites' downlink capacity, Spinlaunch is developing a non-rocket space-launch technology to dramatically reduce costs and shorten timeframes to launch satellites into space, and Locus Biosciences is using CRISPR to develop precision antimicrobials to address antibiotic resistance.

Since inception, Starlight Ventures has invested in more than twenty such companies, with some partners carrying over from previous angel investments. Typical investments start at around a quarter of a million dollars for earlier-stage companies, but the fund plans to follow-on as their companies grow. "We back long-term plays," Patricia says. "After investing in consumer tech for over a decade, shifting towards these sectors has been fascinating and much more purpose-filled. We believe our motivation is shared by the best and brightest entrepreneurs, and therefore believe this is the best place to generate value as well."

[Apply to] starlight.vc; however, a warm intro is highly recommended

[Links] Web: **starlight.vc** Twitter: **@patriciawexler** Medium: **@patriciahalfenwexler**

directory

Startups

Addigy
7315 SW 87th Ave., Suite 200
Miami, FL 33173
addigy.com

Blanket
120 SW 8th St.
Miami, FL 33130
blanket.ai

CarePredict
324 S. University Dr.
Plantation, FL 33324
carepredict.com

Caribu
1951 NW 7th Ave. #600
Miami, FL 33136
caribu.com

ChronWell
150 S Pine Island Rd., Suite 330
Plantation, FL 33324
chronwell.com

DeepBlocks
1035 North Miami Ave.,
Suite 404
Miami, FL, 33136
deepblocks.com

Home61
3401 North Miami Ave.,
Suite 210
Miami FL, 33127
home61.com

Magic Leap
7500 W Sunrise Blvd
Plantation, FL 33313
magicleap.com

Octopi
1010 NE 2nd Ave.
Miami, FL 33132
octopi.os

Plum
11 SW 12th Ave, Suite 104
Dania Beach, FL 33004
plum.wine

SheWorks!
wheresheworks.com

Voyhoy
117 NE 1st Ave.
Miami, FL 33132
voyhoy.com/en

Xendoo
5300 S Powerline Rd.,
Suite 208
Fort Lauderdale, FL 33309
xendoo.com

Programs

500 Startups Miami
111 NE 1st St., 7th FL,
Miami, FL 33132
miami.500.co/miami

Endeavor Miami
121 Alhambra Plaza, Suite 1605
Coral Gables, FL 33134
endeavormiami.org

LAB Ventures
400 NW 26th St.
Miami, FL 33127
thelabmiami.com

Startupbootcamp Scale
Digital Health Miami
1951 NW 7th Ave.
Miami, FL 33136
startupbootcamp.org

**The Women Innovating Now
(WIN) Lab**
Babson College
1200 Brickell Ave., Suite 300
Miami, FL 33131
thewinlab.org/miamiwinlab

The Wynwood Yard
The Lots at 56, 64, 70, 82 NW
29th St.
Miami, FL 33127
thewynwoodyard.com

Venture Café Miami
1951 NW 7th Ave., Suite 600
Miami, Florida 33136
venturecafemiami.org

Spaces

BUILDING.co
120 SW 8th St.
Miami, FL 33130
building.co

Büro
2980 McFarlane Rd.
Coconut Grove,
Miami, FL 33133
buromiami.com

CIC Miami
1951 NW 7th Ave., Suite 600
Miami, FL 33136
cic.com/miami

The LAB Miami
400 NW 26th St.
Miami FL, 33127
thelabmiami.com

Moonlighter
2041 NW 1st Place,
Miami, FL 33127
Moonlighter.co

Pipeline Workspaces
95 Merrick Way, 3rd Floor
Coral Gables, FL 33134
pipelineworkspaces.com

Space Called Tribe
937 NW 3rd Ave.
Miami, FL 33136
spacecalledtribe.com

**WeWork Miami Brickell City
Centre**
78 SW 7th St.
Miami FL, 33130
wework.com

Experts

Cyxtera Technologies
BAC Colonnade Office
Towers
2333 Ponce De Leon Blvd.,
Suite 900
Coral Gables, FL 33134
cyxtera.com

**FIU Miami Urban Future
Initiative**
420 Lincoln Rd. #440
Miami Beach, FL 33139
carta.fiu.edu/mufi

Greenberg Traurig
333 SE 2nd Ave., Suite 4400
Miami, FL 33131
gtlaw.com

Knight Foundation
Suite 3300
200 S. Biscayne Blvd.
Miami, FL 33131-2349
kf.org

**Miami Downtown Develop-
ment Authority (DDA)**
200 S. Biscayne Blvd.
Suite 2929
Miami, FL 33131
miamidda.com

**Nicklaus Children's Health
System**
3100 SW 62nd Ave.
Miami, Florida 33155
nicklauschildrens.org

Radical Partners
1951 NW 7th Ave., Suite 600
Miami, FL 33136
radical.partners

Refresh Miami
refreshmiami.com

SAP Next-Gen
10 Hudson Yards, 48th Floor
New York, NY 10001
sap.com/next-gen

Founders

**BlackTech Week / Space
Called Tribe**
937 NW 3rd Ave.
Miami, FL 33136
blacktechweek.com

Boatsetter
200 SW 1st Ave., Suite #950
Fort Lauderdale, FL 33301
Boatsetter.com

Chewy
1855 Griffin Rd.
Dania Beach, FL 33004
chewy.com

Nearpod
18305 Biscayne Blvd., #301
Aventura,
FL 33160
nearpod.com

WhereBy.Us
1951 NW 7th Ave. #600
Miami, FL 33136
whereby.us

Schools

Code/Art
1951 NW 7th Ave., Suite 600
Miami, FL 33136
code-art.com

**Florida International
University / StartUP FIU**
11200 SW 8th St.
MARC 3rd Floor
Miami, FL 33199
startup.fiu.edu

Ironhack Miami
120 SW 8th St.
Miami, FL 33130
ironhack.com/en

LaunchCode
CIC Miami, 1951 NW 7th Ave.
Miami, FL 33136
launchcode.org

**Miami Dade College
/ The Idea Center**
315 N.E. Second Ave.
Building 8, 5th Floor
Miami, FL 33132
theideacenter.co

**The University of Miami
/ The Launch Pad**
1306 Stanford Dr.
Whitten University Center
#1319
Coral Gables, FL 33146
um.thelaunchpad.org

Wyncode
549 NW 28th St.
Miami, FL 33127
wyncode.co

Investors

Krillion Ventures
2980 McFarlane Rd., Suite 200
Coconut Grove, FL 33133
krillionventures.com

Las Olas Capital Advisors
888 East Las Olas Blvd.,
Suite 200
Fort Lauderdale, FL 33301
lasolasvc.com

Magnetico Ventures
magnetico.vc

Miami Angels
400 NW 26th St.
Miami, FL 33127
miamiangels.vc

Quixotic Ventures
quixotic.ventures

Secocha Ventures
2980 NE 207th St., Suite 502
Miami, FL 33180
secocha.com

Starlight Ventures
starlight.vc

directory

Media Partner

Miami Herald
3511 NW 91 Ave.
Miami, FL 33172
miamiherald.com

Event Partner

eMerge Americas
2333 Ponce de Leon Blvd., Suite 900
Coral Gables, FL 33134
emergeamericas.com

Accountants

BDO Miami
100 SE 2nd St., 17th Floor
Miami, FL 33131
Bdo.com

Canner, Brody & Yan
701 Brickell Ave. #1550
Miami, FL 33131
cpaofmiami.com

Ivy Accounting
777 Brickell Ave. #500,
Miami, FL 33131
ivy-cpa.com

Kaufman Rossin
2699 S Bayshore Dr. #300
Miami, FL 33133
kaufmanrossin.com

MBAF
1450 Brickell Ave., 18th Floor
Miami, FL 33131
mbafcpa.com

PAAST
255 Alhambra Circle, Suite 1100
Coral Gables, FL 33134
Paast.com

Taxfyle
2903 Salzedo St., 2nd Floor
Coral Gables, FL 33134
taxfyle.com

Banks

Banco Sabadell
1111 Brickell Ave. Suite 3010
Miami, FL 33131
Bancosabadellmiami.com

Bank of America
1 SE 3rd Ave.
Miami, FL 33131
bankofamerica.com

Capital One
850 South Miami Ave.
Miami, FL 33130
capitalone.com

Chase Bank
3015 Grand Ave.
Miami, FL 33133
Chase.com

Citibank
201 S Biscayne Blvd., #100
Miami, FL 33131
citi.com

City National Bank of Florida
1450 Brickell Ave., #100
Miami, FL 33131
citynationalcm.com

Regions Bank
3516 Main Hwy.
Coconut Grove, FL 33133
regions.com

Silicon Valley Bank
svb.com

Wells Fargo Bank
169 SW 8th St.
Miami, FL 33130
wellsfargo.com

Coffee Shops and Places with Wifi

ALL DAY
1035 N Miami Ave.
Miami, FL 33136
Alldaymia.com

Capital One Cafe
50 Miracle Mile
Coral Gables, FL 33134
capitalonecafe.com

Eternity Coffee Roasters
117 SE 2nd Ave.
Miami, FL 33131
Eternitycoffeeroasters.co

Juan Valdez
101 NE 2nd Ave.
Miami, FL 33132
juanvaldezcafe.com

Panther Coffee
2390 NW 2nd Ave.
Miami, FL 33127

Pasion del Cielo
3301 NE 1st Ave., #100
Miami, FL 33137
pasiondelcielo.com

Present Bakery
3195 Commodore Plaza
Miami, FL 33133
present-bakery-cafe.business.site/

Starbucks
1080 Brickell Ave., #112
Miami, FL 33130
starbucks.com

Zak the Baker
295 NW 26th St.
Miami, FL 33127
zakthebaker.com

Expat Groups and Meetups

Expats in Miami
facebook.com/groups/miami-expats

French Founders Group
frenchfounders.com

InterNations
internations.org

Israeli American Council
israeliamerican.org/florida

Flats and Rentals

Cervera Real Estate
Cervera.com

Coldwell Banker
coldwellbanker.com

Compass Real Estate
Compass.com

Douglas Elliman
elliman.com

EWM Realty
ewm.com

Fortune International Realty
fir.com

Keller Williams
kw.com

Re/Max
remax.com

Roam Miami
118 SW South River Drive
Miami, FL 33130
roam.co

Important Government Offices

Division of Motor Vehicles
15555 Biscayne Blvd.
North Miami Beach, FL 33160
flhsmv.gov/locations/mi-ami-dade

IRS Miami
51 SW 1st Ave.
Miami, FL 33130
irs.gov

Miami City Hall
3500 Pan American Dr.
Miami, FL 33133
miamigov.com/home

Miami-Dade County Hall
111 N.W. 1st St.
Miami, FL 33128
miamidade.gov/home

Miami Dade Tax Collector
200 NW 2 Ave.
Miami, FL 33128
miamidade.gov/taxcollector

Miami Passport Agency
1501 Biscayne Blvd. #210
Miami, FL 33132
travel.state.gov/content/travel/en/passports.html

Miami Police Department
400 NW 2nd Ave
Miami, FL 33128
miami-police.org

US Citizenship & Immigration Services
8801 NW 7th Ave.
Miami, FL 33150
ucis.gov

Insurance Companies

Allstate
allstate.com

Brown & Brown
bbmia.com

CHUBB
Chubb.com

Geico
geico.com

Progressive
Progressive.com

State Farm Insurance
statefarm.com

Willis Towers Watson
willistowerswatson.com/en

Language Schools

Berlitz Language Center
1200 Brickell Ave., #502
Miami, FL 33131
berlitz.us

EC English Language Schools
1111 Lincoln Rd., #301
Miami Beach, FL 33139
Ecenglish.com

Inlingua Language School
80 SW 8th St., #1720
Miami, FL 33130
inlingua-if.com

Kaplan International Miami
4425 Ponce De Leon Boulevard
Coral Gables, Miami, FL 33146
kaplaninternational.com

Language On Academy
1201 Brickell Ave., #620
Miami, FL 33131
languageonschools.com/locations/miami/

OpenEnglish
2901 Florida Ave.
Suite 840
Coconut Grove, FL
Openenglish.com

Open Hearts Language Academy
825 Brickell Bay Dr., #1850
Miami, FL 33131
ohla.com

TALK English Schools
1390 Brickell Ave.
Miami, FL 33131
talk.edu/english-schools/miami

Startup Events

BlackTech Week
blacktechweek.com

Creative Mornings
creativemornings.com/cities/mia

The LAB Events
https://www.thelabmiami.com/upcoming-events

Startup Grind Miami
startupgrind.com/miami

unbound Miami
unbound.com

glossary

A

Accelerator
An organization or program that offers advice and resources to help small businesses grow

Acqui-hire
Buying out a company based on the skills of its staff rather than its service or product

Angel Investment
Outside funding with shared ownership equity

API
Application programming interface

ARR
Accounting (or average) rate of return: calculation generated from net income of the proposed capital investment

Artificial Intelligence
The simulation of human intelligence by computer systems; machines that are able to perform tasks normally carried out by humans

B

B2B
(Business-to-Business)
The exchange of services, information and/or products from a business to a business

B2C
(Business-to-Consumer)
The exchange of services, information and/or products from a business to a consumer

Blockchain
A digital, public collection of financial accounts in which transactions made in bitcoin or another cryptocurrency are recorded chronologically

BOM
(Bill of Materials)
A list of the parts or components required to build a product

Bootstrap
To self-fund, without outside investment

Bridge Loan
A loan taken out for a short-term period, typically between two weeks and three years, until long-term financing can be organized

Burn Rate
The amount of money a startup spends

Business Angel
An experienced entrepreneur or professional who provides starting or growth capital for promising startups

Business Model Canvas
A template that gives a coherent overview of the key drivers of a business in order to bring innovation into current or new business models

C

C-level
Chief position

Cap Table
An analysis of ownership stakes in a company

CMO
Chief marketing officer

Cold-Calling
The solicitation of potential customers who had no prior interaction with the solicitor

Convertible Note/Loan
A type of short-term debt often used by seed investors to delay establishing a valuation for the startup until a later round of funding or milestone

Coworking
A shared working environment

CPA
Cost per action

CPC
Cost per click

Cybersecurity
Technologies, processes and practices designed to protect against the criminal or unauthorized use of electronic data

D

Dealflow
Term for investors that refers to the rate at which they receive potential business deals

Deeptech
Companies founded on the discoveries or innovations of technologists and scientists

Diluting
A reduction in the ownership percentage of a share of stock due to new equity shares being issued

E

Elevator Pitch
A short summary used to quickly define a product or idea

Ethereum
A blockchain-based software platform and programming language that helps developers build and publish distributed applications

Exit
A way to transition the ownership of a company to another company

F

Fintech
Financial technology

Flex Desk
Shared desk in a space where coworkers are free to move around and sit wherever they like

I

Incubator
Facility established to nurture young startup firms during their first few months or years of development

Installed Base
The number of units of a certain type of product that have been sold and are actually being used

IP
(Intellectual Property) Property which is not tangible; the result of creativity, such as patents and copyrights

IPO
(Initial Public Offering) The first time a company's stock is offered for sale to the public

K

KPI
(Key Performance Indicator) A value that is measurable and demonstrates how effectively a company is achieving key business objectives

L

Later-Stage
More mature startups/companies

Lean
Refers to 'lean startup methodology;' the method proposed by Eric Ries in his book for developing businesses and startups through product development cycles

Lean LaunchPad
A methodology for entrepreneurs to test and develop business models based on inquiring with and learning from customers

M

M&A
(Mergers and Acquisitions) A merger is when two companies join to form a new company, while an acquisition is the purchase of one company by another where no new company is formed

MAU
Monthly active user

MVP
Minimum viable product

O

Opportunities Fund
Investment in companies or sectors in areas where growth opportunities are anticipated

P

P2P
(Peer-to-Peer) A network created when two or more PCs are connected and sharing resources without going through a separate server

Pitch Deck
A short version of a business plan presenting key figures generally to investors

PR-Kit (Press Kit)
Package of promotional materials, such as pictures, logos and descriptions of a company

Product-Market Fit
When a product has created significant customer value and its best target industries have been identified

Pro-market
A market economy/a capitalistic economy

S

SaaS
Software as a service

Scaleup
A company that has already validated its product in a market and is economically sustainable

Seed Funding
First round, small, early-stage investment from family members, friends, banks or an investor

Seed Investor
An investor focusing on the seed round

Seed Round
The first round of funding

Series A/B/C/D
The name of funding rounds that come after the seed stage

Shares
Units of ownership of a company that belong to a shareholder

Solopreneurs
A person who sets up and runs a business on their own and typically does not hire employees

Startup
Companies under three years old, in the growth stage and becoming profitable (if not already)

SVP
Senior Vice President

T

Term Sheet/Letter of Intent
The document between an investor and a startup including the conditions for financing (commonly non-binding)

U

Unicorn
A company often in the tech or software sector worth over US$1 billion

USP
Unique selling point

UX
(User experience design) The process of designing and improving user satisfaction with products so that they are useful, easy to use and pleasurable to interact with

V

VC
(Venture Capital) Financing from a pool of investors in a venture capital firm in return for equity

Vesting
Process that involves giving or earning a right to a present or future payment, benefit or asset

Z

Zebras
Companies which aim for sustainable prosperity and are powered by people who work together to create change beyond a positive financial return

STARTUP GUIDE TRONDHEIM   The Entrepreneur's Handbook
STARTUP GUIDE HAMBURG   The Entrepreneur's Handbook
STARTUP GUIDE LUXEMBOURG   The Entrepreneur's Handbook
STARTUP GUIDE VIENNA   The Entrepreneur's Handbook
STARTUP GUIDE TEL AVIV   The Entrepreneur's Handbook
STARTUP GUIDE MADRID   The Entrepreneur's Handbook
STARTUP GUIDE VALENCIA   The Entrepreneur's Handbook
STARTUP GUIDE COPENHAGEN   The Entrepreneur's Handbook
STARTUP GUIDE PARIS   The Entrepreneur's Handbook
STARTUP GUIDE REYKJAVIK   The Entrepreneur's Handbook
STARTUP GUIDE STOCKHOLM   The Entrepreneur's Handbook
STARTUP GUIDE MUNICH   The Entrepreneur's Handbook
STARTUP GUIDE FRANKFURT   The Entrepreneur's Handbook
STARTUP GUIDE ZURICH   The Entrepreneur's Handbook
STARTUP GUIDE LONDON   The Entrepreneur's Handbook
STARTUP GUIDE LISBON   The Entrepreneur's Handbook
STARTUP GUIDE NEW YORK   The Entrepreneur's Handbook
STARTUP GUIDE BERLIN   The Entrepreneur's Handbook
STARTUP GUIDE OSLO   The Entrepreneur's Handbook

→ startupguide.com   Follow us

About the Guide

Based on traditional guidebooks that can be carried around everywhere, Startup Guide books help you navigate and connect with different startup scenes across the globe. Each book is packed with useful information, exciting entrepreneur stories and insightful interviews with local experts. We hope the book will become your trusted companion as you embark on a new (startup) journey. Today, Startup Guide books are in twenty different cities in Europe, the US and the Middle East, including Berlin, London, New York, Tel Aviv, Stockholm, Copenhagen, Vienna, Lisbon and Paris.

How we make the guides:

To ensure an accurate and trustworthy guide every time, we team up with a city partner that is established in the local startup scene. We then ask the local community to nominate startups, coworking spaces, founders, schools, investors, incubators and established businesses to be featured through an online submission form. Based on the results, these submissions are narrowed down to the top hundred organizations and individuals. Next, the local advisory board – which is selected by our community partner and consists of key players in the local startup community – votes for the final selection, ensuring a balanced representation of industries and startup stories in each book. The local community partner then works in close collaboration with our international editorial and design team to help research, organize interviews with journalists as well as plan photoshoots with photographers. Finally, all content is reviewed, edited and put into the book's layout by the Startup Guide team in Berlin and Lisbon before going for print in Berlin.

Where to find us: The easiest way to get your hands on a Startup Guide book is to order it from our online shop: startupguide.com/books

If you prefer to do things in real life, drop by one of the fine retailers listed on the stockists page on our website.

Want to become a stockist or suggest a store?

Get in touch here: sales@startupguide.com

The Startup Guide Stores

Whether it's sniffing freshly printed books or holding an innovative product, we're huge fans of physical experiences. That's why we have stores in Berlin and Lisbon and we're opening a third store in Copenhagen in November 2018. Not only do the stores showcase our books and a range of curated products, they're also our offices and a place for the community to come together and share wows and hows. Say hello!

Lisbon:
Rua do Grilo 135, 1950-144 Lisboa
Mon-Fri: 10h-19h
+351 910 781 512
lisbon@startupguide.com

Berlin:
Waldemarstraße 38, 10999 Berlin
Mon-Fri: 10h-18h
+49 (0) 30 374 68 679
berlin@startupguide.com

Copenhagen:
Borgbjergsvej 1, 2450 København, Denmark
Mon-Fri: 10h-17h
+45 52 17 85 45
copenhagen@startupguide.com

#startupeverywhere

Startup Guide was founded by Sissel Hansen in 2014. As a publishing and media company, we produce guidebooks and online content to help entrepreneurs navigate and connect with different startup scenes across the globe. As the world of work changes, our mission is to guide, empower and inspire people to start their own business anywhere. Today, Startup Guide books are in 18 cities in Europe, the US and the Middle East, including Berlin, London, New York, Tel Aviv, Stockholm, Copenhagen, Vienna, Lisbon and Paris. We also have two physical stores in Berlin and Lisbon which double as offices for our 20-person team.
Visit our website for more: startupguide.com

Want to get more info, be a partner or say hello?

Shoot us an email here info@startupguide.com

Join us and #startupeverywhere

Miami Advisory Board

With thanks to our **Content Partners**

IIMIAMI**DDA**
DOWNTOWN DEVELOPMENT AUTHORITY

Nicklaus Children's Health System

Our Event Partner

And our **Media Supporters**

Miami Herald

Event Partner
/ eMerge Americas

eMerge Americas is a two-day annual global technology conference where entrepreneurs, investors, executives, government officials and thought leaders from around the world convene in Miami to discuss technologies transforming industries. The next edition takes place from April 29–30, 2019 at the Miami Beach Convention Center.

The concept for eMerge Americas came about after serial entrepreneur Manuel "Manny" Medina had sold his data services company Terremark to Verizon in 2011. While thinking about how to give back to the community in Miami and reflecting on how frustrating it was for him to always go to technology conferences outside of the city, the idea of a technology conference came to mind. After two years of planning and developing the event alongside his daughter Melissa, the inaugural eMerge Americas conference came to life in 2014.

eMerge Americas' signature event is about connecting the entrepreneurial ecosystems in the US, Latin Americas and Europe, as well as providing Miami startups with access to global enterprises, mentors, investors and the movers and shakers in the international scene. The conference consists of multiple stages where attendees can hear from industry experts and inspiring thought leaders, participate in a hackathon, watch a Startup Showcase and take part in several networking events. "Our mission is to make sure that we're helping foster the Miami entrepreneurial ecosystem as much as we possibly can," says Melissa Medina, president at eMerge Americas.

Previous speakers include Steve Wozniak (cofounder of Apple Computer), Melissa Barnes (managing director, LATAM and Canada, of Twitter) and Vicente Fox (former president of Mexico). In April 2018, the event hosted over fifteen thousand attendees from more than forty countries. "I believe eMerge Americas will help in continuing to change mindsets as well as to amplify the message that Miami does in fact have an incredibly vibrant entrepreneurial ecosystem," says Melissa. "The success of eMerge Americas has truly been because it's a community effort and because we've received support from organizations such as Knight Foundation. Everybody works together and is clearly on the same page with the same mission."

Media Partner
/ Miami Herald

Long before the commercial success of enhanced-reality firm Magic Leap and pet-supplies retailer Chewy.com, the *Miami Herald* championed entrepreneurship in South Florida. In 1998, the company launched the *Miami Herald* Business Plan Challenge to encourage and recognize startups in Miami-Dade and Broward counties. In the years since, the *Herald* has steadfastly tracked this burgeoning sector through columns, magazine articles and live events, and through partnerships with locally based efforts such as the eMerge Americas conference.

Today, the Kaufmann Foundation ranks the Miami region as number one in the nation for startup activity. But the ecosystem is still young. Venture funding, training and talent acquisition, mentorship and scaling are still challenges. The *Herald* does its part by covering local startups and the efforts by many organizations – including Knight Foundation, Endeavor, Cambridge Innovation Center, The Lab and educational institutions – to enhance opportunities for success.

The *Herald* continues to recognize and encourage innovation and entrepreneurship through the *Miami Herald* Startup Pitch Competition, the successor to the original business plan challenge. This extensive program encompasses competitive tracks for teens, university communities and individuals throughout the South Florida community by inviting participation and highlighting promising startups in the verticals most critical to the local economy: healthtech, bioscience, hospitality, travel, tourism, logistics and trade, real estate and financial technologies.

WHERE NEXT?